MELANIA

Skyhorse® and Skyhorse Publishing® are registered trademarks of Skyhorse Publishing, Inc.®, a Delaware corporation.

10 9 8 7

Library of Congress Control Number: 2024944380

Print ISBN: 978-1-5107-8269-3
Ebook ISBN: 978-1-5107-8270-9

Printed in the United States of America

Contents

Author's Note   VII

Chapter 1: USA   1

Chapter 2: The Win   5

Chapter 3: April 26, 1970   10

Chapter 4: Lights, Camera, Model   21

Chapter 5: "Hi, I'm Donald Trump."   35

Chapter 6: All Business   58

Chapter 7: It Is Official   63

Chapter 8: Why Was the Speech Not Vetted?   68

Chapter 9: On My Way   76

Chapter 10: My Husband, the President   82

Chapter 11: In the White House   88

Chapter 12: Welcome to the White House   102

Chapter 13: Be Best   106

Chapter 14: Going Global   115

Chapter 15: Moments of Crisis   136

Chapter 16: 2020   146

Chapter 17: Fostering the Future   166

Chapter 18: "Good Luck and Be Safe"   178

Photo Credits   184

MELANIA

Author's Note

Dear Reader,

Writing this memoir has been a deeply personal and reflective journey for me. Throughout my life, I have witnessed many extraordinary events and have met incredible people. There have been moments of joy and triumph, as well as challenges and heartaches. In sharing my story, I hope to show you the woman behind the public persona, to illuminate the values and experiences that have shaped me, and to offer insights into the complexities of life in the public eye. It is my sincere wish that you will find inspiration in my journey, recognizing the universal themes of resilience, love, and the pursuit of one's dreams.

I believe it is important to share my perspective, the truth, especially in these times of division and uncertainty. As a private person who has often been the subject of public scrutiny and misrepresentation, I feel a responsibility to set the record straight and to provide the actual account of my experiences. My hope is that by sharing my story, I can contribute to a greater sense of understanding and hope for the future among us all.

Sincerely,

Melania

Chapter 1

USA

"Prepare for landing . . ." the pilot announced. I pressed the off button on my Walkman and gazed out the window, hoping to catch a glimpse of New York City in the distance. My heart pounded with excitement. I was twenty-six years old, and while I had traveled everywhere in Europe, I had never been on a journey quite like this.

This was America . . . New York! A different world altogether.

I had made the decision to test my skills in the American modeling market carefully, after weighing all the professional and personal implications. There were risks, yes, but buoyed by an internal sense of confidence and the ongoing support of my family, I was certain I could succeed. The potential rewards would outweigh the uncertainties.

I had embraced such risks many times in the past, but this gamble felt more significant. I packed my apartment in Paris, met with my agent in Milan, and said goodbye to my family in Slovenia. My life was now two suitcases and a carry-on, containing only essentials: clothing, shoes, cosmetics, my passport, and my portfolio. The portfolio, a culmination of nearly a decade of dedicated modeling work across Italy, France, and Germany, was my most valued asset.

Ten hours before touching down in New York, I had checked my suitcase at Linate Airport in Milan where I navigated through the noisy crowds of tourists, all returning home at the end of the European summer holiday. It felt as though I was swimming against the tide, moving in the opposite direction of everyone around me.

In Europe, where traveling between countries is commonplace, I was at home anywhere on the continent. Which was precisely why leaving and embracing a new challenge felt exhilarating and exciting. But the distance between America and Europe felt immense and my family and I had found these goodbyes particularly difficult. Still, I was grateful for their trust, which strengthened my decision, and motivated by their encouragement. "Good luck," they said, as we hugged. We held each other tightly. "Be safe. Let us know when you arrive."

As I boarded the plane, I thought of them and fingered a necklace they had given me engraved with the German words "*Ich liebe dich*"—I love you. I carried their love with me as I stepped into the unknown.

Tuesday afternoon . . . JFK Airport. The airport was crowded. After a long walk, I finally reached immigration and customs. There were two lines: one for US citizens, and one for visitors. I joined the visitors' line, which moved significantly slower than the other one as the guards meticulously examined every detail of each passenger's papers, holding up passports, tilting their heads to the left and right, flipping pages, and deciphering stamps. Some of the people ahead of me had trouble that needed sorting out, which slowed things down even further. The line was crawling. I waited patiently. There were twenty people ahead of me at first. Then ten . . . five . . . two. . . . Finally, it was my turn. The agent waved me to the booth. He didn't say much, but he looked me up and down, up and down. He checked back and forth between my passport photo and the face in front of him. I felt confident. My documentation was in order, and my English was proficient.

"First time here?" he asked. "Yes," I said. "First time."

He smiled at me, stamped my passport, and handed it back to me. I looked at the date: August 27, 1996.

"Welcome to the United States," he said.

Despite the fog of jet lag, I recognized the importance of this moment. My life had shifted direction, presenting new opportunities, and I was ready to embrace the path ahead.

After retrieving my luggage, I proceeded to the exit. The heat and humidity enveloped my face. The sound of honking vehicles filled the air, accompanied by a persistent haze of exhaust fumes. I stood by the curb and concentrated on locating the driver sent by the agency, scanning the crowd for any sign of him. Just as I wanted to turn away to find a phone booth to make a call, a long black limousine arrived, and the driver lowered the window.

"Melania Knauss?" he asked.

"Yes. Hello. Are you from Metropolitan Models?" I inquired.

"Yes, ma'am."

He opened the door. I stepped into the back seat. I felt a sense of relief to be away from the noisy chaos of the curb. The interior of the limousine exuded elegance. I felt an immediate sense of comfort and ease.

Within a minute we were on the road. The din of JFK faded into the background, and I finally took a deep, calming breath.

Traffic was heavy on the way into the city, so it took a while before the skyline came into view. When it did, my heart leapt. The Empire State Building, the Chrysler Building, and the Twin Towers stood proudly against the horizon. Having only seen this iconic view in magazines and films, witnessing it in person was exhilarating. The scale and vibrancy of Manhattan were overwhelming, and with each passing moment, my excitement grew. Any second thoughts about my decision to come here dissipated; this is where I was meant to be.

Reflecting on that pivotal day in my life, I recognize the profound significance of that decision to move to New York. Now I am struck by my youthful confidence! Life's circumstances shape you in many ways, often entirely beyond your control—your birth, parental influences, and the world in which you grow up. As an adult, there comes a moment when you become solely responsible for the life you lead. You must take charge, embrace that responsibility, and become the architect of your own future. Coming to America, coming to New York City? That was my moment.

Another pivotal moment came as I raised my right hand and recited the Pledge of Allegiance, ten years after my initial arrival, in July 2006, and became an American citizen.

It was not an easy process. And my personal experience dealing with the trials of the immigration process opened my eyes to the difficulties faced by all who wish to become US citizens. I felt a sense of pride and accomplishment. Reaching the milestone of American citizenship marked the sunrise of certainty.

I had become a true citizen of the world, at home wherever I was. And now, with gratitude—in my heart and on paper—I was, finally, also an American.

Chapter 2

The Win

On the morning of Tuesday, November 8, 2016, I had gotten up early. The city was quiet, calm. I love early, peaceful mornings—peace I would especially need in the coming hours. Barron was still asleep when I entered his room and gave him a gentle kiss on the forehead. Taking an extra moment to look at him, knowing his world had already undergone so much transformation since his father's decision to run for president, I realized this day would begin changes none of us could predict. I made a commitment then and there that if we were headed to the White House, I would fiercely protect my beautiful son in every way I could.

Donald had poured his heart and soul into building a movement that could bring about real change. The campaign had grown into a powerful force, driven by his vision, plus the support of the American people. Now, it was up to the American people to decide if they would trust my husband to lead our country. We had done everything we could to convince the public that Donald was the right choice to be our nation's 45th president, and for now, there was nothing left to do but wait—and vote.

At 10 a.m., Donald and I made our way downstairs and passed a large group of supporters on the street who were waiting for a glimpse of us as we left Trump Tower. The air was filled with the resounding cheers of "TRUMP! TRUMP! TRUMP!" as we stepped into the car. The motorcade moved slowly, drawing the attention of New York City as we passed by.

When Donald and I arrived at the voting station, we discovered another significant gathering of admirers, journalists, and law enforcement officials. Plus a few dissenters, of course. I was pleased to hear my name also being cheered, amid the clamor. This Manhattan scene was a true testament to the passion, commitment, and enthusiasm of our incredible fan base and supporters across America.

Inside the polling station, election workers greeted us. We entered the privacy of the voting booth. Standing beside my husband and seeing his name on the ballot, I felt a surge of pride and amazement. It was a moment filled with emotion and significance for me, representing yet another peak of our journey together so far.

I marked my ballot for Donald Trump, then took a moment to land back on Earth where I could carefully consider the other races. After my husband waited patiently for his methodical wife, we walked together to submit our ballots. Handing over those pieces of paper, we completed a significant step in the American democratic process that I had grown up admiring from afar, a process I was now squarely in the middle of, a process that would soon thrill me, and sometimes in the coming years, confuse me—like it did millions of other Americans.

By noon, we were back home at Trump Tower, waiting impatiently for the election's outcome. With little to do until the results began to trickle in later that evening, we entered a new phase of anticipation. In the wake of our morning's frenzy, I carried on with my usual responsibilities, knowing that the outcome was ultimately in the hands of the

American people. While I was hoping for a victory for Donald, I had also prepared myself for the possibility of a different result. Regardless of the outcome, I knew that my family and I would be just fine.

I devoted time that day to Barron and my parents; I knew Donald was busy going to his campaign office, then home again, then the office again. Each time we were together that day, I was impressed by his calm. He was focused and relaxed. This man is remarkably confident under pressure, and the pressure test was just beginning.

By 7 p.m., the major polls and pundits had all but crowned Hillary the victor, and our family waited, along with millions of others, to see if they were right. But as the evening progressed, the mood began to shift. Donald gained momentum in key battleground states, surprising many who had predicted a different outcome. By 10 p.m., it became clear that this election would not be as straightforward as had been initially reported by the media. Excitement filled the room as the results continued to come in in Donald's favor. The media, the pollsters, the pundits—they had all gotten it wrong. Donald was defying the odds, inching closer to victory. And then, it was official. At 2:30 a.m., Wisconsin's results confirmed it: Donald had won the presidency. The room erupted in a mix of cheers, gasps, and hugs. The world as we knew it was about to change. What an extraordinary moment it was. I vividly recall Bret Baier's announcement, "The president-elect is Donald J. Trump." We were momentarily speechless, absorbing the weight of what had just transpired.

"Can you believe it!?" Donald's voice reflected a mix of astonishment and excitement as he hugged me. "Can you believe it?" I responded, "Of course I can!" I'd believed in his victory all along, knowing his unwavering dedication to making America great again.

Despite the late hour, we made our way to the Hilton Hotel, where Donald would deliver his victory speech. The atmosphere was electric as we waited for Hillary Clinton to concede the election. Finally, at 2:40 a.m. the call came in, and within a few moments Donald took the stage. Barron and I stood beside him, proud and ready for the next chapter.

"I've just received a call from Secretary Clinton," he said. "She congratulated us on our victory, and I congratulated her and her family on a very, very hard-fought campaign. Now it's time for America to bind the wounds of division; we have to get together. To all Republicans and Democrats and independents across this nation, I say it is time for us to come together as one united people."

Donald struck the perfect tone, transitioning from his combative campaign persona to a unifying leader. He recognized the need for healing and unity in America. It was a moment that showcased his ability to rise above partisanship and bring the country together.

"It's time," he said. "I pledge to every citizen of our land that I will be president for all Americans, and this is so important to me. For those who have chosen not to support me in the past, of which there were a few people, I'm reaching out to you for your guidance and your help so that we can work together and unify our great country. . . . As I've said from the beginning, ours was not a campaign, but rather an incredible and great movement made up of millions of hard-working men and women who love their country and want a better, brighter future for themselves and for their families. . . . It's a movement comprised of Americans from all races, religions, backgrounds, and beliefs who want and expect our government to serve the people and serve the people it will. . . . We're going to get to work immediately for the American people. And we're going to be doing a job that hopefully you will be so proud of your president. You'll be so proud. Again, it's my honor. It was an amazing evening. It's been an amazing two-year period. And I love this country."

While the joy of our victory was overwhelming, my mind quickly shifted to the multitude of tasks before us, as I contemplated the weight of responsibility and the challenges that lay ahead. I also couldn't help but think about Barron and how this new stage in our lives would impact him. As I considered the many roles I now had to balance—mother, wife, First Lady, daughter, sister, friend—I knew that careful planning and organization would be key in navigating this new journey. The media's scrutiny only added to the weight of these responsibilities, but I was determined to rise to the challenge and ensure that our family transitioned smoothly into our new reality.

I finally closed my eyes around 5:00 a.m. and opened them just two hours later. In the half-light of the morning, my thoughts turned to my own journey as an American, born far away, like so many others.

Chapter 3

April 26, 1970

My mother, Amalija, was born on July 9, 1945, in the Austrian town of Judendorf-Straßengel, where her family, like so many others, had been displaced during the turbulent years of World War II. Although they faced challenges, my grandfather Anton, a skilled shoemaker and innovative farmer, never lost sight of his dreams.

When they returned to their village of Raka, nestled in the serene countryside just south of Sevnica, Anton wasted no time in pursuing his passion for agriculture. It was here that he would go on to breed a culinary masterpiece—the renowned *raska čebula,* or Raka onion, a sweet red variety that quickly became a favorite among the Slovenian people.

From a young age, my mother's innate talent and boundless creativity as an artist, patternmaker, and tailor shone brightly. It came as no surprise that when she finished Fashion Design and Pattern School, she was handpicked to join the design studio of the Jutranjka children's clothing factory in Sevnica, a mere twenty minutes from her hometown. At Jutranjka, my mother was the artisan behind the scenes, transforming the designers' sketches into exquisite patterns fit for the runway. With impeccable taste and confidence, she took pride in her work, thriving in the world of fashion.

My mother was the epitome of elegance. She often emphasized that self-care was essential not only to a person's well-being but also to being able to effectively care for others, and she instilled this conviction in me from an early age, teaching me the importance of attending to one's appearance before venturing into the world. I have always found joy in the process of making myself presentable and getting ready.

"If I don't take care of myself," she would say, "how would I know how to care for others?" The value of self-care remains a guiding principle in my life.

My father, Viktor, was confident and industrious and had a strong desire to explore new destinations. He had an outgoing personality and was known for his ability to connect with others. In my childhood memories, he is constantly moving and working with those around him.

Much like my mother, my father hailed from a lineage of hardworking and enterprising Slovenians. My father's roots can be traced back to the town of Radeče, just a stone's throw away from Sevnica. Despite the tumultuous times brought on by war, my grandfather managed to secure a position as production manager at the local Piatnik factory, allowing the family to weather the war. Born on November 23, 1941, in the midst of the German occupation, my father was christened Viktor Waldemar Knaus.

My father's passion for automobiles and motorcycles was a love affair that began in his youth and blossomed into a lifelong devotion. His expertise in all things mechanical was unmatched, and he could effortlessly repair and enhance any vehicle.

Starting out as a driver in the Yugoslavian Army, he honed his skills behind the wheel and quickly advanced to chauffeuring high-profile individuals, such as the mayor of a nearby town.

He met my mother in 1966, when his career trajectory shifted toward a new direction. Transitioning from a driver to a sales professional at Slovenija Avto, he quickly ascended the corporate ladder. His drive propelled him to great heights within the company, securing his reputation as a respected and influential figure in the industry. Following the independence of Slovenia, my father seized the opportunity to realize his lifelong dream of owning his own business. Through hard work, perseverance, and a deep-rooted passion for all things automotive, my father would go on to build a successful career and business.

My parents married in a civil ceremony and held their reception at the Podvin Castle. However, my mother, a true traditionalist, longed for a Catholic wedding to honor her devout upbringing. And so, a few months later, they renewed their vows in the St. Lawrence Church in my mother's hometown.

While my parents lived through significant political events, filled with the echoes of communism, the Cold War, and the enigmatic figure of Tito, they were not particularly politically active themselves. Despite Slovenia being part of communist Yugoslavia, the communism there was different from that of the Soviet Union. Growing up, I felt more connected to our neighbors in Italy or Austria than to other communist countries in Eastern Europe.

The Slovenian people have historically held a strong sense of independence and self-reliance. In Slovenia, individuals were rewarded for their hard work and talent. Rules, while always present, did not dictate every aspect of daily life. My family, like many others, prospered due to my parents' ambition, determination, and strong work ethic. The

Slovenia of my childhood felt unrestrictive, emphasizing the value of hard work and individual responsibility.

Sevnica, the town of my childhood, was a picturesque place nestled on the banks of the Sava River. Surrounded by a lush green forest of pine and fir, it was a storybook setting for a happy upbringing. The medieval castle overlooking the old town, the winding roads of the valley, and the quaint churches scattered throughout the landscape were all familiar sights that filled my childhood with warmth and fond memories.

Thanks to the beautiful taste and creative vision of my mother, our home was a vibrant and lively place. Despite the plain exterior of our three-bedroom apartment, my mother's artistic touch brought character to every corner of our living space. The emerald green and burgundy red walls of the kitchen and a striking blue accent wall in the living room served as testaments to her bold and imaginative design choices. She infused our home with love and warmth.

My mother described me as a joyful and contented baby, noting my delight in playing with Barbie and dressing her in handmade outfits. This playtime activity brought me hours of enjoyment and fostered my imagination. I also loved a red race car model gifted to me by my father. It was a treasured memento from the thrilling Formula 1 races he would take us to. This token sparked my interest in cars and racing, instilling in me a sense of excitement and adventure.

Another significant aspect of my life has always been music, even from a very young age. While listening to my favorite records, I would immerse myself in the delightful stories and gorgeous illustrations of my Marinka books, allowing myself to be transported to a magical land that fueled my imagination and encouraged me to dream big.

During my early childhood, while many of my peers attended kindergarten, I was fortunate to have a private nanny who cared for my sister and me. She crafted beautiful birthday cakes for me and my family that were not only visually stunning—adorned with handmade sugar flowers—but also very flavorful.

In retrospect, these childhood experiences shaped my creativity, resourcefulness, and love of the arts and exploring the world.

M

Whether heading to Milan for modeling opportunities, traveling to Ljubljana for school, or simply running errands around town, my father and I created lasting memories during our drives together. Each trip deepened our connection, and I was always eager for these drives, as they symbolized freedom and stirred my admiration for the precision, luxury, and innovation of automobiles. Thanks to my father, I developed a profound knowledge of the mechanical and technological aspects of cars.

One of my fondest memories is when my father brought home a stunning French Citroën Maserati SM. I was seven years old, and to me it was the most beautiful car I had ever seen—sleek, sporty, and a luxurious, rich coffee brown. The next day, my father took all of us out for a drive. I still remember the smell and feel of the new leather as I climbed into the back seat. Over the years, my father assembled a collection of exquisite vehicles: Ford Mustangs, German BMWs, and a Ford Cougar XR7, alongside a selection of prestigious Mercedes-Benzes. Yet, none could rival the sheer thrill of that Citroën Maserati SM. I can still feel the rush of excitement, sitting behind my father, soaking in every moment, my heart racing, as he unleashed its power. It was pure adventure, a connection forged on the open road, a taste of freedom.

As a child, I demonstrated a strong sense of organization, orderliness, and methodical approach in all my projects. I possessed a keen curiosity and diligent work ethic. I had a genuine passion for learning and delved into subjects ranging from art and history to geography. My fascination with different cultures and distant lands led me to pick up phrases in various languages during family travels, including German, Italian, and even Russian, which I studied in school for a period of time.

As a hard worker, I was always striving for the best. I understood from a young age that studying and learning were the keys to success, and I took great pride in consistently earning good grades. As a young teen, I participated in gymnastics and played basketball and handball. On the weekends, my father taught my sister Ines and me tennis. I tried to strike the ball with all my strength using a wooden tennis racket.

The only thing I recall abandoning was the guitar, which I'd desperately wanted to master until I experienced significant discomfort in my fingertips during my initial lessons. My fingers ached so much that I came home from the lesson and told my parents I didn't want to continue. Despite reassurances from them that the pain would soften as my fingertips hardened, I chose to discontinue. While I acknowledge that I am capable of many things, I determined that the guitar was not meant for me.

Overall, my childhood experiences shaped me into a disciplined, ambitious individual who values hard work, dedication, and self-awareness. I continue to approach tasks with a methodical mindset, striving for excellence in all that I do.

Life, of course, presented its fair share of challenges. As a child I cherished solitude and found solace in the company of my family or in my own thoughts. I often found myself navigating the world on my own terms.

I learned that regardless of the circumstances or the company I found myself in, the most crucial relationship I could cultivate was the one I had with myself. Each individual is on their own unique journey, and it is essential to be grounded in one's own identity and values. I embrace my individuality and confidently walk my own path.

Young people can be so dismissive toward anyone who is different in any way. Kids can be cruel to each other; it seems almost inherent in human nature. Every generation experiences the "mean kids" in school. I was often targeted for my appearance, being perceived as "too" tall and "too" skinny. I undoubtedly stood out. In retrospect, I realize that most of this behavior was fueled by their insecurities.

Back then the term "bullying" wasn't commonly used, but some of the behavior likely qualified. Personally, I managed to rise above these challenges, maintaining a strong sense of self and confidence in my accomplishments. I would simply shrug and think, "Whatever! It's their problem, not mine."

If Facebook, Twitter, and TikTok had existed back then, the dissemination of opinions and criticisms would likely have been amplified, leading to immediate and far-reaching negative comments. This could have significantly shaped public perception and the conversation about me. I often wish children could experience life without social media platforms, to know the joy of genuine connections, and the freedom to explore the world without the constant noise of online comparison.

I have come to understand that genuine happiness is not found in material possessions, but rather in the depth of self-awareness and self-acceptance. This realization has become my compass, leading me toward a life enriched with authenticity, confidence, and inner peace.

M

As a young girl, I held my older sister, Ines, in high regard. She had a unique blend of seriousness and playfulness that I admired. Ines excelled academically with apparent ease, showcasing a natural intellect and curiosity about the world around her. Her artistic talents were evident from a young age, as she effortlessly created beautiful works of art. Ines was an excellent communicator with a vibrant energy that drew people toward her, making friends with ease. Her passion for dance, design, and painting was nothing short of awe-inspiring. Ines was more than just a sister to me; she was a guiding light who illuminated my path and inspired me to reach for the stars.

Growing up, Ines and I shared a close bond that revolved around our mutual love for music, design, literature, and fashion history. Ines, being older than me, introduced me to a world of creativity and expression that shaped my interests. Our nights were often spent staying up late, listening to music on our record player, and discussing the latest trends. We were immersed in the music of iconic artists such as the Bee Gees, Donna Summer, and Pink Floyd, all the big artists from the 1980s. Later, when MTV began broadcasting in Slovenia, we eagerly awaited the latest music videos, just like kids in New York or London.

One of the most memorable experiences we shared was attending our first concert together, Elton John's European Express Tour, on April 19, 1984. I was just shy of fourteen years old, filled with excitement as our parents, who were going to the concert too, drove us from Sevnica to the big arena in Zagreb. While they took their seats, Ines and I made our way all the way to the stage. The show was nothing short of spectacular, with Elton John captivating the audience with timeless hits such as "Tiny Dancer," "Rocket Man," and "Crocodile Rock" and his dazzling stage presence. The costumes, the sunglasses, the lights! The energy in the arena was incredible.

A few years later, Ines invited me to join her to visit the captivating city of Venice. The picturesque canals, elegant gondolas, and remarkable museums and architecture profoundly impressed me. And in

1990, we attended another concert, this time Tina Turner. We danced and sang along to all of her songs. It was an unforgettable evening.

The experience of traveling with Ines is one that I will always cherish. It not only introduced me to the outside world but also solidified the connection we shared as siblings.

As a child, my perception of the world was limited to the experiences within my own family. The routines and activities that defined my daily life seemed completely normal to me. From the warmth of my mother's creativity, to my father's busy professional life, and my close relationship with my sister, everything felt like an integral part of the fabric of our existence.

The simple pleasures of family dinners, weekend visits to our grandparents in Raka or Radeče, and travels to different places felt like the natural rhythm of our lives. Whether it was the short walk to school or the occasional concert in Croatia, these experiences were the building blocks of our shared family life. It was only later, as I grew older and gained a broader perspective, that I came to appreciate the effort and sacrifice that went into creating these moments of joy and togetherness.

Looking back, I now understand the hard work and dedication that my parents invested in shaping our family life. Their commitment to providing us with a stable and nurturing environment, filled with love and opportunities for growth, laid the foundation for the person I have become. I am grateful for the values they instilled in me and the memories we shared, which continue to shape my worldview and guide my actions to this day.

Growing up in Eastern Europe, I never felt isolated or limited in my experiences. Despite living in a region that was often seen as separate from the rest of the world, we were fortunate to have the opportunity to travel and explore different cultures. With Venice just a three-hour drive away and Vienna within easy reach, we were constantly exposed to the beauty and culture of neighboring countries.

Whether it was skiing in the Alps or visiting the charming city of Trieste, each trip was a chance to learn, grow, and appreciate the world around us.

Even the border crossings, with their meticulous customs checks, were just part of the experience. We embraced the challenges and uncertainties, knowing that they were a small price to pay for the incredible memories we would create.

Among the most cherished experiences of my youth were our annual summer trips to the Dalmatian coast of Croatia. The picturesque towns of Split, Zadar, and Dubrovnik left an indelible mark on me. I can still vividly recall running barefoot on cool, polished cobblestone streets, worn smooth by the passage of countless generations. In the evenings, we would venture out for gelato, the sea breeze carrying the sweet scent of the ocean. The sound of music drifted through the air, creating a harmonious backdrop to the laughter of children playing in the streets. These moments filled me with a sense of freedom and wonder. The world seemed limitless, brimming with love and beauty. To this day, the memories of those summer trips to the Dalmatian coast remain etched in my mind as a reminder of the simple joys that life has to offer.

My father documented our lives with a video camera from birth, capturing moments that we would later watch. The images flickered on a large white wall, cast there from a standalone projector. These family screenings brought us joy and laughter, strengthening our connection and preserving our cherished memories.

Returning home to Sevnica was always a solace for me. The familiarity of our bright house—designed and built by my parents—the aroma of my mother's cooking, and the engaging conversations with my sister served as reminders of the love and warmth that defined our family. Despite the challenges and uncertainties of the outside world, coming back to our lives, just the four of us, was a constant source of happiness and contentment.

Countless stories about my childhood have been published, yet they often miss the mark, painting a bleak and inaccurate picture of my upbringing. In truth, my childhood was filled with happiness, beauty, and positivity, far from the typical narrative of a girl raised in a communist society. I was fortunate to have people in my life who taught me the importance of dreaming big and working diligently to achieve my goals.

My parents served as a profound source of inspiration for me, both individually and as a united front. Their strong work ethic, commitment to family, and passion for creativity were foundational pillars in their relationship. Their untiring dedication to each other and to our family was evident in every aspect of their lives. Their example continues to guide and motivate me in my own life.

Chapter 4

Lights, Camera, Model

It started with a glamorous adventure, a train ride through the picturesque landscapes of Croatia and Serbia, heading toward the city of Belgrade, where my mother had invited me and my sister Ines to model her latest creations on the runway. The anticipation of stepping into the world of fashion at six years old filled me with excitement and joy. With a heart full of love for fashion and admiration for my mother, I jumped at the chance.

The venue was bustling with excitement as people gathered for the show. The runway was set up in the center of the hall, with parents and children preparing backstage. My mother helped us get ready in our first outfits of the day before leading us to the runway. She whispered a few words of encouragement, and we were off, gliding down the runway, showcasing our outfits. It was a thrilling experience, and I felt proud to be a part of the show.

After finishing my first round on the runway, I promptly headed backstage to change into the next outfit. This process repeated itself multiple times as I modeled raincoats, dresses, and blouses with a big smile on my face. I lost count of the outfits I wore that day, but the experience was truly enjoyable.

M

As I matured, my focus shifted from modeling to creating. While many of my peers opted for a high school closer to home, I was drawn, much like Ines, to something more stimulating and challenging. My parents shared this sentiment, and I was determined to push myself. My mother always emphasized the importance of curiosity and ambition in building a fulfilling life, one step at a time.

Ines had gained entry to the renowned Secondary School for Design and Photography in Ljubljana at just fifteen. Admission was fiercely competitive, with only a select few students accepted each year. Following in Ines's footsteps, I faced the challenging entrance exam two years later.

Passing the exam, I eagerly accepted my spot at the school and began making plans to move there for the upcoming school year. I chose to pursue a degree in industrial design, a field that combines my interests in art, fashion, graphic design, interior design, and production. This program required a blend of creativity, discipline, and structure, which aligned perfectly with my skills and goals.

I have always valued my independence, so when the opportunity arose to move to a big city, I was eager to branch out. My parents were supportive of my decision, understanding the importance of fostering my success.

My parents had purchased an apartment in Ljubljana for Ines three years prior to provide her with a comfortable place to study and for our family to have a place to stay when visiting the city. I was excited at the prospect of living independently for the first time, while also having the comfort of being with my sister. It was the perfect arrangement.

Ljubljana was an exciting city—full of energy and new impressions, fueling my growing sense of curiosity. I approached my new environment with a desire to learn and absorb as much as possible.

School was demanding, requiring Ines and I to dedicate a significant amount of time to studying. We were only fifteen and seventeen, but we were focused on shaping our futures.

M

In 1987, a year after I relocated to Ljubljana, my mother invited me to accompany her to a fashion show she was attending. I happily accepted the invitation and was looking forward to the experience. After the show, I took a moment to step outside and enjoy some fresh air while waiting for my mother to finish her conversation with her colleagues. In the crisp January air of Slovenia, I stood in a white ensemble made by my mother. As I waited, a man approached me. Introducing himself as Stane Jerko, a photographer, he proposed the idea of capturing some photographs.

"You're beautiful," he said. "I think you'd make a great model."

In that moment, as a young teenager, I couldn't help but feel a sense of doubt. I accepted his contact information, but I felt unsure of his intentions.

I had previously been photographed for children's clothing catalogs and runway shows, as well as by my sister, who took photography classes. However, I had never modeled for a professional photographer before. Given my academic obligations, having my pictures taken was not a priority for me at the time.

During a conversation with my sister, I mentioned the encounter, and Ines said that the photographer's name sounded familiar to her. We discovered that he was well-known for his work in *Jana* magazine, Slovenia's premier lifestyle publication. The thought of collaborating with him was intriguing, but I didn't want to go alone.

"Let's go together," Ines, always a trusted companion, said.

The studio was hardly glamorous. It was located in a modest Ljubljana building and lacked all of the amenities typically found at a photo shoot, such as a makeup artist or hair stylist, but my sister and I remained focused on the task at hand. With just a photographer and a white backdrop, we were able to create strong images. The simplicity of the setup allowed for my natural beauty to shine through without the need for elaborate outfits, hair, or makeup.

After changing into a Jane Fonda–style bodysuit that I had brought with me and a pair of leg warmers, a popular look in the 1980s, I proceeded to try on a few dresses that were scattered around the studio. There were no shoes, so I remained barefoot for most of the photos.

While the shoot was more casual, the photographer seemed pleased with our results.

I had to rely on his expertise and experience, as he was well established in Slovenia. Overcoming my initial uncertainty, I trusted that he knew what he was doing.

The photo shoot at the studio was an unremarkable experience. Overall, it was an afternoon spent capturing images, but nothing extraordinary. The lack of preparation and organization during the photo shoot was somewhat disappointing. As a perfectionist, I prefer things to be thoughtful and well-planned. Without professional assistance for hair and makeup, no designated outfits or even a changing area, and a photographer snapping photos without a clear direction, my expectations were not very high.

I was not informed about the intended use of the photos or who they would be shared with. There was no formal agreement in place, and no compensation.

It appears, though, that the photos were circulated. I began receiving offers for modeling assignments. I signed with an agency which led to more significant bookings, including features in a Slovenian fashion magazine and participation in runway shows. I was proud of my early success, but still saw modeling as a hobby rather than a career. My primary focus was my studies, and I had now set my mind on becoming an architect. I took the rigorous entrance exam for the faculty of Architecture at the University of Ljubljana and was accepted.

In an unexpected turn of events, I met an Italian movie producer while doing a fashion show in Trieste. Intrigued by my look, he invited me to a modeling contest held in Italy to discover a new "face for the movies," which presented an exciting opportunity for aspiring talents. The contest was organized and hosted by Cinecittà, the renowned European film studio, and the winner would not only receive a generous prize but also secure a part in a movie. While I had never considered a film career, the competition seemed worth exploring.

I arrived in Italy on a Wednesday in the middle of September, ready to take on the competition that awaited me. As I observed the other girls tirelessly practicing their runway walks, I felt a sense of calm confidence wash over me. I knew I was destined to do well at the big runway event on Friday night. The competition was fierce, but I was ready to showcase my elegance and poise. As I watched the other contestants, I decided to simply be myself, believing my authenticity would shine through. I chose to embrace my uniqueness and trust in my capabilities, knowing that success would follow.

The preshow interviews with the judges on Friday provided an opportunity to share background personal information, including details about our lives, origins, interests, and educational backgrounds. Following the interviews, it was time to demonstrate our talents on the runway. I felt self-assured in the elegant long black dress I had chosen for the occasion.

As I walked the runway, the judges watched with keen eyes, scrutinizing my every move. Their pens sketched out notes on their pads, capturing each detail of my performance. The audience watched quietly as I strutted confidently in my high heels.

And . . . I won.

The crowd erupted as I walked back onto the runway, holding a beautiful white poodle on a leash. The photographers snapped away, capturing the moment while the spectators were shouting "Brava! Bellissima! Brava!"

I was elated by the news that I had won first place on the grand international stage. The sheer magnitude of it all left me in awe.

As I stood there at center stage, I was showered with gifts. A bouquet of flowers, a gleaming silver plaque, a stunning painting of the castle, and an envelope filled with my prize money.

"Let us capture this incredible moment!" the photographers shouted. I handed over my winnings to an organizer for a quick photo op. However, when my belongings were returned, the envelope containing the prize money was conspicuously missing. I inquired about its whereabouts, only to be met with confusion and ignorance. The money had inexplicably disappeared, leaving me feeling betrayed by the individuals I had placed my trust in. As a renowned studio, Cinecittà should have upheld a higher standard of professionalism. The loss of the money itself was insignificant compared to the breach of trust that occurred.

I returned home with a sense of disappointment, not in the amount lost, but in the manner in which it had been callously stolen from me.

A week later, an organizer reached out to me, extending an invitation to return to Rome and collaborate with their studio.

"We would like you to come back," he said. However, my response was a resounding "no." I had no desire to associate with individuals of such a deceitful nature. The lesson I learned from that experience is far more valuable than any material reward. Such dishonesty has no place in my life, and it never will.

M

By 1992, at the age of twenty-two, I was a dedicated architecture student and a successful part-time model. One day, Ines, who was a student at the Academy of Fine Arts at Edward Kardelj University in Ljubljana by now, told me about a Slovenian modeling contest called the "Look of the Year," organized by *Jana* magazine. The winner would secure a modeling contract with Metropolitan Model Agency, a prestigious Paris-based agency.

Ines urged me to submit my photos. "No one looks like you," she said. I had already made a name for myself in the industry, having impressed audiences in Italy and graced the runways, magazines, and catalogs of Slovenia, but was wary of entering another competition.

After much consideration, I decided to submit my photos. I quickly received an invitation.

When I arrived in the seaside town of Portorož for the contest, I couldn't ignore the buzz surrounding another contestant who seemed to have the right connections. Despite the talk, I was determined to focus on my performance, maintain professionalism, and hopefully establish some valuable contacts during the event.

My instincts were correct; the other model won first place. But I came in second and was offered a contract with RVR, a modeling agency in Milan.

This unexpected opportunity forced me to make a decision between pursuing a career in architecture or modeling. Despite the difficulty of the choice, I trusted in my abilities and believed that I would be successful no matter which path I chose.

On the day of my move to Milan, I was filled with anticipation and excitement for the new chapter ahead. Leaving behind my family and the architecture and design school I had worked hard to be a part of was a significant step, but I was ready for the challenge.

Moving to a new country, learning a new language, and embarking on a new career were intimidating, but I was determined to succeed. The responsibility for my success now rested solely on my shoulders, and I was prepared to take on the challenge with determination and perseverance.

During my first weeks I quickly realized that I was solely responsible for navigating my way through this new environment. I was on my own . . . all alone on trains, on planes, in hotels, and on the busy streets of the city, surrounded by strangers, walking quickly on my way to my next appointment. The solitary life didn't bother me; I was used to being on my own and had always enjoyed my own company. In fact, the solitude helped clarify my outlook. I embraced it as an opportunity for introspection and growth. It was a challenge to be in a new city with a new career—but I was determined to work as hard as possible to achieve my goals.

With the "Look of the Year" contest, I had secured a contract with an agency in Milan, but soon it became clear to me that my aspirations were set higher than what was being offered. I made the bold decision to switch agencies in pursuit of opportunities that truly matched my vision and potential. In the world of modeling, settling for anything less than excellence was simply not an option.

If I sought to elevate my modeling career, I knew I needed to align myself with one of the best agencies in the industry. Riccardo Gay was a legend in 1992, known for working with top photographers and representing elite models.

I got a number from one of the models at the casting call, called the agency, and asked for a meeting. When I arrived, the receptionist ushered me into Riccardo's Gay office. He greeted me with a smile and offered me a seat opposite him. As I watched him silently leaf through the pages of my portfolio, I was aware that the photos were not the highest quality, and that the shoots I had done were not for the most prestigious clients. After a few minutes, he closed the book and looked up at me. "I would love to represent you in my agency," he said.

He graciously introduced me to his colleagues, who welcomed me with open arms and invited me to tour their headquarters. I maintained a composed demeanor, though internally I was filled with elation. Securing a modeling contract with this esteemed agency through my determination and drive was a momentous achievement for me.

Somtimes, in order to succeed, you must be willing to take risks and make tough decisions. You need to trust yourself and your abilities, and never settle for anything less than what you deserve. The path to success may not always be easy, but with determination and courage, you can achieve your dreams.

Soon, my schedule was filled with go-sees, test photography, casting calls, and exciting photo shoots. From the cobblestone streets of Portofino for an editorial shoot, to the historic beauty of Florence for an advertising campaign, to posing for a Japanese lingerie catalog in a Milan studio, the world of high fashion was now my playground, and I was living out my dreams. My future was taking shape, and I would not be deterred by the harsh realities of the modeling world. Despite the glamorous aspects of the industry, such as exotic locations, beautiful clothes, and talented photographers, all models deal with frequent rejection. For every job secured by one model, hundreds of others are turned away. Sometimes, the client would be looking for a blonde, sometimes a brunette. Sometimes, you're too skinny; sometimes, you're too curvy. Sometimes—many times—there's no discernible reason at all. Your exterior is judged constantly. It is a brutal criticism that comes with being a model. To survive in the industry requires a high level of confidence, resilience, and determination.

I understood that setbacks were to be expected and was intent on never taking rejection personally. At the end of the day, if I didn't land a job, I understood that it had little to do with who I was as a person. I maintained a positive attitude and stayed dedicated to my craft, focused on delivering high-quality work. I made sure to be punctual, prepared, and professional in providing photographers with the shots they required. The high-stakes world of modeling in Milan demanded a constant balancing act between the glitz and the grit.

Models were often invited to parties and clubs by groups of men, promising work, money, or connections. It was common for agents to extend invitations for trips, dinners, or parties, emphasizing the importance of networking in the industry. While others indulged in a lifestyle of excess, I stayed focused on my goals and ambitions. I witnessed the harmful effects that drugs and excessive drinking had on young women around me, and I refused to be swayed from my path, remaining singularly intent on my career goals. In hindsight, I am proud of weathering these challenges by staying true to myself and remaining focused.

I was convinced I had made the right choices.

M

After two successful years in Milan, I decided to take on a new challenge and relocate to Paris. The fashion market in Paris was known for its competitiveness and high standards, making it the perfect place for me to further develop my career. I was excited for the opportunities that came with working in the world capital of high fashion. In Paris, the market was even more exclusive, with haute couture at every corner and prestigious clients waiting to be impressed. The competition was fierce, but the rewards were even greater.

At that time, the modeling industry favored a very slim look, particularly on runways. As someone with a curvier physique, I focused my efforts on commercial modeling, catalogs, advertisements, and television commercials.

By the mid-1990s I had built a successful career in Europe. At the casting call in Milan, I met Paolo Zampolli, co-owner of Metropolitan Models in New York. During our meeting, he expressed interest in having me come to the United States to discuss potential opportunities with his agency. I found him to be straightforward and serious, qualities that I valued in a professional partner.

His keen interest in my portfolio and his proposal to join his agency in New York left me intrigued and filled with anticipation for what lay ahead. The prospect of expanding my horizons in the glamorous world of New York City modeling was hard to resist.

I had worked hard to build a reputation for professionalism, skill, and a strong work ethic, and I was determined to take my career to new heights in New York. It was time to test my skills in the biggest and most exciting modeling market in the world.

M

I found myself utterly enamored with the pulse of New York City. It resonated with me from the very beginning—the fast tempo and the positive energy. Each corner turned revealed a new side of New York's multifaceted personality, from the chic boutiques on Madison Avenue to the busy streets in the Financial District.

While I occasionally yearned for the refined charm of European cities, there was a raw, modern elegance in New York's towering skyscrapers and sleek architecture that captivated me.

Clad in a pair of flats, I carried my modeling portfolio and high heels, ready to conquer whatever challenges awaited me. And as I continued to navigate its streets and avenues, I knew that this city would forever hold a special place in my heart.

After securing my work visa, my professionalism and punctuality won over clients, leading to bookings with prestigious department stores like Bergdorf Goodman and Neiman Marcus and editorial shoots for magazines such as *Fitness* and *Glamour*. Embracing my maturity and refined look, I secured steady work, navigating the competitive modeling industry with grace.

When not in front of the camera, I attended meetings and networked with photographers. New York demands constant motivation and drive. Success in this industry is achieved through self-motivation and perseverance. While supported by a team of professionals, it was ultimately my determination that pushed me to reach new heights.

M

After a few months of renting a room that the agency provided me, I found myself a one-bedroom on the third floor of a historic brownstone building near 30th Street and Park Avenue: A place of my own. It was charming and bright, with simple moldings and brown wooden floors. There was a view of the courtyard and a big tree in the middle of it. I loved this touch of nature in the middle of the concrete jungle. The agency was in Union Square, and many of the go-sees and studios were downtown, so living in Midtown meant I could walk almost everywhere.

I always made time in my schedule to enjoy the city's cultural gems: the Museum of Modern Art, the Guggenheim, and the Metropolitan Museum of Art. Visiting museums is a habit I have maintained in every city I've lived in. They bring me joy and inspiration.

New York City was a vibrant and sophisticated playground. Memorable dinners at Cipriani in Soho with friends and fellow models were a social highlight.

Living and working in New York was an exhilarating experience, filled with constant opportunities. The city's fast pace fueled my drive, keeping me motivated as I booked jobs, shot campaigns, and sought new projects. Modeling was far from a nine-to-five job; my schedule was packed, but the thrill of being in demand and always on the move was energizing.

Navigating the glamorous yet challenging fashion world in New York required willpower and stamina. Despite setbacks, I remained dedicated and true to my values. While some industry encounters were difficult, I handled them with poise.

Rejections did not deter me; they only fueled my desire to excel. I traveled to Europe for prestigious shoots, then to San Francisco for Macy's, to Miami for *Elle Canada*, making my mark in the industry.

My life at that time was not perfect, but filled with moments of success and achievement. Although I faced rejections in my career, I remained dedicated and fiercely focused on my goals. I took risks fearlessly, guided by my youthful courage. In hindsight, I realize that it was this boldness that paved the way for my triumphs.

What I accomplished in that first year felt extraordinary. I was living confidently in a foreign land, completely independent and self-reliant. It was a bold move to venture to New York, but it was a risk worth taking. While I could have settled for a comfortable career in Slovenia, Milan, or Paris, my inner voice urged me to strive for more. My journey to New York was a testament to my firm determination, courage, and resilience.

Through it all, I was blessed with the steady support and encouragement of my parents and sister back home. While it was challenging to stay connected in the mid-1990s, we managed to keep in touch through phone calls. My family's pride in my achievements was a constant source of motivation. One day, as I was out walking in Midtown, I looked up and caught sight of my larger-than-life image on a billboard in Times Square. In that moment, a surge of pride washed over me, knowing that my work had paid off in the most rewarding way.

Chapter 5

"Hi, I'm Donald Trump."

On a Friday night in September 1998, as I settled into the comfort of my New York City apartment after a whirlwind trip to Paris, my phone rang. It was a friend of mine.

"My boyfriend is throwing a party at the Kit Kat Klub tomorrow night," she said. "Please come. We haven't seen each other in so long."

"I just got back from Paris," I said.

"Please, it will be fun. A lot of people will be there. We'll pick you up."

While I was tired and jetlagged, I loved the idea that my weekend was about to be filled with the company of friends.

I have always been selective in how I choose to spend my time and where I put my energy. A late-night party at the club was not my top choice for a Saturday evening. I much preferred staying in, watching a film, or going to dinner with close friends. Though I didn't shy away from social gatherings, clubs were simply not my cup of tea.

I accepted the invitation anyway; after all, it was Fashion Week—a time of glamour and sophistication. I was actually looking forward to mingling with industry insiders and trendsetters.

When I stepped into the sleek black limo my friend arrived in, I felt like a celebrity en route to a gala. As we arrived at the Kit Kat Klub, the energy of the crowd and the dazzling lights greeted us. Inside, the dark, crowded space buzzed with models, photographers, editors, and designers mingling on this Fashion Week Saturday night. I settled in upstairs at our table in the VIP section, where the atmosphere was one of sophistication and camaraderie. Some guests danced, while others engaged in lively conversation, and we were all enjoying ourselves.

I saw my friend wave at someone behind me. When I turned around, I noticed a man and an attractive blonde woman approaching us.

"Hi. I'm Donald Trump," the man said when he reached my table. "Nice to meet you." I recognized the name, and I knew he was a businessman or celebrity, but not much else. He put his hand out to shake mine.

"Hello," I replied. "I'm Melania."

His eyes filled with curiosity and interest, and, seizing the opportunity, he took the seat next to mine and started a conversation. He asked me about my time in New York, my Slovenian home, and my world travels. It was a moment of connection, a brief encounter that left a lasting impression. It was nice to make a new acquaintance.

He was accompanied by a beautiful date, so I initially dismissed our conversation as mere pleasantries exchanged at an industry event. The music was loud, and the crowd boisterous, making it difficult to truly connect with someone.

From the moment our conversation began, I was captivated by his charm and easygoing nature. There was so much bustling activity around us, but his intent focus on our interaction made me feel like the center of his world. It was a refreshing departure from the usual superficial small talk, and I found myself drawn to his magnetic energy.

When his companion left for a moment, he asked me for my phone number. I politely declined his request. He was a little surprised.

"Give me *your* number," I said.

"I'll give you my number," he said, "if you promise to call me."

With a hand gesture, Donald called over his bodyguard. His big shoulders leaned in as he listened to him, before discreetly writing a note on a sleek business card. Donald took the card and handed it to me.

"Call me," he said with a smile.

I tucked the card into my clutch before his date returned to the table.

"Nice to meet you," he said before making his way to the exit, stopping to talk to a few people on the way out.

As I packed for my Caribbean photo shoot the next day, Donald's image danced through my mind. His polished business look, witty banter, and obvious determination fascinated me. The thought of contacting him added a sense of anticipation to returning.

After a successful shoot on the island, I returned to my apartment, eager to unwind and relax. As I unpacked, I came across the card, which had two handwritten numbers. Curious, I dialed the first number—his home. After three rings, his voice greeted me on the answering machine.

"Hello, it's Melania. I promised to call you. I hope you are well," I said before leaving my number.

He called me back that evening after 9 o'clock. "Why didn't you call sooner?" he asked. "I was thinking about you."

It was that same voice—warm, friendly, strong. He sounded happy that I actually called him.

"I was away," I said. "I just got back home."

"You should have called me earlier. I was at another party and would have loved to have taken you with me."

"I'm sure you had a nice date," I said teasingly. He laughed.

We had an easy conversation that evening, discussing my travels. Though we made no definitive plans, I found great pleasure in our exchange. The connection between us was palpable, much like what we had shared the week prior.

"I would love to see you," he said before we hung up. His words were so genuine and warm. We both had hectic schedules, but I knew we would make it work.

I was pleasantly surprised by a call from Donald the next day, inviting me on a weekend drive to his property in Bedford, New York. His voice was confident when he extended the invitation. I accepted, and I looked forward to seeing him again.

It was a crisp September Sunday when Donald picked me up in his black Mercedes. Traffic was light on the way out of the city. We chatted about our lives, our dreams, and our experiences. He was so easy to talk to and genuinely interested in everything. He told me all about his business and his love for golf. It was refreshing to meet someone so successful yet down-to-earth. It was a beautiful ride, just the two of us. His love for driving was obvious, and I shared that same passion. When I first arrived in New York, one of my first priorities was obtaining my driver's license. Driving provides freedom, which I always treasure.

The house in Bedford sits on 230 acres of land at the end of a long driveway. The house was built in 1919.

"It's like a French chateau," I said. "It's beautiful. Do you live here?"

"No, I don't actually live here. I'm just here to make sure everything is ok," he said with a smile. He mentioned his plans to maybe turn the property into a golf club and how he liked to personally check on his projects. We walked through the rooms, him giving me a tour while also inspecting the place. Looking back, it was a very "Donald" kind of first date—a mix of business and pleasure. It was clear that his work was his passion; he didn't separate it from the rest of his life. It was all just one big, exciting thing to him. I found that aspect of him intriguing right from the start. I think he appreciated that I had knowledge and experience under my belt. Maybe he saw me as someone he could have more in-depth conversations with? It was nice to feel like we were on the same wavelength. Perhaps he saw me as more of a peer than the women he was used to spending time with.

I didn't really think of it as a "date," just spending time with someone intriguing. During our lunch, Donald casually mentioned his children, and shared some details of his family life. He told me that he was separated and in the process of divorce from his second wife, the mother of his youngest daughter. I refrained from passing any judgement, choosing instead to enjoy his company.

He was a bit older than me, but I, at the age of twenty-eight, felt an instant connection with him. As someone who had traveled the globe and encountered many types of people, I found Donald to be different, a breath of fresh air. His work ethic and success were admirable. He projected a sense of authenticity. He had a zest for life that was infectious. He was successful and hardworking, but also so down to earth and real. I really liked that about him.

After returning home, I was giddy with joy. It's truly a rare feeling to instantly connect with someone on such a deep level. I was immediately at ease in Donald's company, as if our souls had known each other for a long time. Our chemistry was undeniable, and our connection felt natural.

As I got to know him better, I realized the public only saw a part of Donald Trump. In private, he revealed himself as a gentleman, displaying tenderness and thoughtfulness. For example, Donald to this day calls my personal doctor to check on my health, to ensure that I am okay and that they are taking perfect care of me. He isn't flashy or dramatic, just genuine and caring.

As Donald and I spent more time together in late 1998 and early 1999, I made a conscious effort to maintain a sense of privacy in our relationship. The press followed him around constantly. I wasn't one for seeking attention, so I tried to keep our time together as low-key as possible. I just wanted to enjoy getting to know him without all the outside noise.

In the early days of our courtship, our love was a well-kept secret known only to the two of us. It was exciting and romantic, and I'll always treasure that unhurried and unforced time at the beginning of our journey together.

When we were in New York, we often enjoyed our time in a private club downtown, catching up with friends for dinner. Other times, we would go to the movies and Broadway shows or stay in, watching TV, or listening to music.

We share a love for Elvis Presley and Elton John. Whenever he had music playing at home, he'd crank up the volume and pull me into a spontaneous dance. And when it came to movies, we enjoyed everything from westerns to old classics to dramas. His taste was eclectic, just like mine.

We visited the theater regularly, seeing almost every new release. Our evenings were filled with the excitement of baseball games, football games, and boxing events.

It wasn't all entertainment. I was drawn to Donald's organizational skills, his mindset, and his good taste, which was evident in every aspect of his being. It was a clear reflection of not only his self-respect but also his profound respect for those in his presence. It was his way of expressing, "I value your time as much as my own." We agreed on living a healthy life, evident in our abstinence from alcohol and tobacco. We had so much in common and I had no doubts about him, but I believed in taking things one step at a time in our relationship. We both agreed to take the time to get to know each other gradually, ensuring that we were truly aligned. Despite my best attempts at discretion, it was only a matter of time before the public got wind of our romance. As a figure of prominence, Donald thrived in the spotlight, enjoying every opportunity to be seen and meet people. Soon, we were attending high-profile events like the MTV Video Music Awards, the Grammys, and the Oscars together. I wasn't as accustomed to the spotlight as he was, and it was an exhilarating time for us. As our relationship garnered more attention, I could sense the increased scrutiny. It was an unusual experience. Everywhere we turned, people sought to uncover the details of our relationship. The media's fascination was both flattering and annoying.

They couldn't see past our twenty-four-year age difference. The gossip columns labeled me a "gold digger," insinuating my affection for him was solely motivated by his wealth. Such baseless accusations could never tarnish the love and connection we shared. I was already a thriving model, enjoying my success when our paths crossed. I had earned my fortune and could have easily captured the attention of numerous celebrities if I had so desired. His age was never a concern for me. His energy and zest for life made us feel we were on the same wavelength.

I entertained setting the record straight but recognized the challenges of doing so. To engage in such matters—to dignify each and every untruth—would be squandering my time and energy, for no minds would be swayed, no opinions altered. I instead focused my time and energy on more productive endeavors and rose above the falsehoods. As a model, I had encountered many who believed they had me all figured out, assuming they knew every detail of my life. However, my interaction with Donald took this to a new extreme.

I have chosen to maintain a more discreet presence in the public eye, in stark contrast to Donald. I have always prized my privacy and opted for a more selective lifestyle. At the same time, I have never felt the need to dictate Donald's actions, as I am not one to exert control over anyone. I value autonomy and believe in allowing people to live according to their wishes. Donald's candid approach to dealing with the public and the media is commendable, displaying a fearless confidence in expressing his views. While our viewpoints may differ, he has always respectfully welcomed my opinions. Our mutual understanding and appreciation for each other's perspectives create a harmonious relationship.

By 2004, I had established a robust career as a model. Donald and I were six years into our relationship. I had moved into Donald's residence in Trump Tower a couple of years earlier, and we had created a happy life together. I took pleasure in cooking for him, supporting him in his daily routines, and maintaining a beautiful home. It was my priority to safeguard his welfare, meticulously attending to every aspect of his life. Donald and I share a deep appreciation for the finer things in life. Sometimes he seeks my opinion on matters of style, which I am always happy to provide, even if he elects to go his own way in the end.

One evening in April 2004, Donald and I were preparing to attend the prestigious Met Gala, a key fundraising event for the Costume Institute of the Metropolitan Museum of Art. Under the leadership of *Vogue*, the event had become a must-attend for celebrities from the worlds of fashion, Hollywood, and high society.

I was all set in a stunning Versace couture dress that Donald had purchased for me at a charity auction. As we were about to leave, Donald, looking dapper in his tuxedo, surprised me with a beautiful emerald-cut diamond ring set in platinum. "I love you," he whispered softly. "I want to spend the rest of my life with you."

My heart was ready to burst. "Yes," I replied, feeling like the luckiest woman in the world. Little did I know he had been planning this moment for weeks, waiting for the perfect opportunity to ask me to be his forever. It was April 26, my birthday, and I had just turned thirty-four. With the gorgeous ring on my finger, we went to the gala, hand in hand, ready to embark on this new chapter of our lives together.

The sparkling ring went unnoticed by many that night, but the news of our engagement soon appeared in the pages of the *New York Post*: "DONALD MERGING—TRUMP TO MARRY MODEL MELANIA."

Following our engagement, the wedding planning process took off at an accelerated pace.

Donald and I scheduled our wedding for January 22, 2005. The ceremony would take place at the Episcopal Church of Bethesda-by-the-Sea in Palm Beach, followed by a reception in the new ballroom at Mar-a-Lago, which Donald was racing to complete in time.

The event was to be a lavish affair, with every element radiating sophistication and glamor. The beige, gold, and white color palette would create an ambiance that set the tone for the evening. Instead of the conventional round tables, I specifically chose long tables decorated with elaborate candelabras and gorgeous flowers. The seating arrangement for the five hundred celebrity guests had to be carefully curated, ensuring an enjoyable experience for all.

My parents were visiting from Slovenia, and I was grateful for my mother's keen eye for detail as she joined my perfect team to assist with planning the event. Donald expressed his confidence in my abilities and jokingly mentioned that he would simply show up when I instructed him to.

I assured him that everything would be perfect.

Shortly after my engagement, I received a call from Anna Wintour at *Vogue*, inviting me to meet with her to discuss an exciting new idea. During our meeting in her New York office, she proposed a magazine cover and feature story on me and my wedding.

I was delighted by Anna's invitation to fly me to Paris to assist me in selecting a wedding dress, particularly with the respected *Vogue* editor André Leon Talley accompanying us.

Our first visit, to the Valentino and Chanel showrooms in Paris, offered a unique glimpse behind the scenes of the world of high fashion. But I knew exactly what I wanted for my wedding dress, so with that vision in mind, I sought out the legendary Dior designer John Galliano, whose work I had long admired. I was immediately taken by his fearless creativity and open spirit. One of the couture dresses that was being modeled at the runway captivated me, and I knew he was the ideal designer for this important collaboration.

"This one is incredible," I murmured to André when the model walked past us. The strapless Dior gown, adorned with fifteen hundred pearls and rhinestones, was a true masterpiece. With its thirteen-foot train and sixteen-foot veil, the dress weighed nearly sixty pounds. I instantly knew it was the one.

Although my wedding was grand in scale, including the global media coverage, what I felt in my heart was what every other bride feels on her special day. The pressure to ensure everything went smoothly was certainly real, but ultimately, my primary focus was on celebrating Donald and my love and commitment, surrounded by my loved ones.

Just before the ceremony, as I stood in the corridor on a blissful evening, a sense of serenity washed over me. I was grateful for the warm Florida winter night adding a touch of magic to the occasion, and the presence of my parents, my sister—who was my maid of honor—Donald's children, and our closest friends.

With a soaring rendition of "Ave Maria" sung by Camellia Johnson I made my entrance down the aisle. My father beamed with pride as he joined me, guiding me toward the altar.

Our exchange of vows in the ornate church was deeply meaningful. Donald sealed our union three times, with each kiss more tender than the last. Next to the altar, we lighted my baptism candle. This cherished heirloom, brought from my hometown by my beloved mother, held a significance beyond words. My mother's thoughtful gesture, honoring our heritage, added a deep sense of tradition to our special day. The candle symbolized the enduring union between past and present. Lighting that same candle once again at our son's baptism in 2006, the flame of tradition burned brightly in our hearts.

As we exited the church and slowly proceeded down an open-air corridor toward our awaiting Maybach, we were greeted by cheers from our guests and onlookers. With excitement, we began our first journey as husband and wife. Our next destination was a celebration at the gorgeous Mar-a-Lago.

The ballroom had been completed on schedule, just in time to accommodate our five hundred guests. The atmosphere was lively as Basketball legend Shaquille O'Neal, boxing promoter Don King, former president Bill Clinton and US senator Hillary Clinton, political figures Rudy Giuliani and George Pataki enjoyed the music of the Michael Rose Orchestra, along with their caviar and champagne.

Members of the media Barbara Walters, Anna Wintour, Chris Matthews, Matt Lauer, Gayle King, Simon Cowell, and Kelly Ripa were chatting and enjoying each other's company. The atmosphere in the room was electric, and I felt a sense of pride in the successful outcome of the wedding.

As dinner was served, I gazed out at the beautiful ballroom, lit by towering candelabras and studded with gorgeous floral arrangements. It was a sight to behold, elegant and dramatic in every way. And the culinary creations by Chef Jean-Georges Vongerichten were nothing short of spectacular. From the delicate shrimp salad to the perfectly cooked beef tenderloin, every bite was a true masterpiece of taste and presentation.

The grand finale of the evening was a magnificent seven-tier golden sponge cake, adorned with delicate handspun sugar roses. This confection stood almost five feet tall and weighed a staggering two hundred pounds. It was truly a work of art.

The evening was made even more special when, to everyone's surprise, legendary singers Tony Bennett, Paul Anka, and Billy Joel took the stage to serenade the crowd with a series of love songs. Billy Joel gave a special rendition of "The Lady Is a Tramp," humorously changing the lyrics to reference Donald Trump. While everyone moved to dance outside Mar-a-Lago, I changed into a stunning white Vera Wang dress. The party by the pool carried on into the late hours, filled with dancing and laughter.

For our honeymoon, Donald and I decided to stay in the paradise of our own home, as we spared ourselves the hassle of extensive travel. While we had enjoyed many of the world's most exotic destinations, we found true serenity in the comfort and splendor of our own backyard. For us, there was no place more idyllic than right where we were, together.

M

"You are going to be a daddy!" I burst out when Donald returned home from work one night in July 2005.

His face lit up with joy. "That's amazing! Wonderful!" he exclaimed. We were both over the moon. After allowing the news to settle in, I reached out to my sister to share the joy, followed by my parents in Slovenia. Apart from a select few family members and close friends, we opted to keep the news private for the time being. Pregnancy speculations had been circulating since our wedding, and I wanted to shield our future child from becoming a topic of tabloid gossip. While the news would eventually be made public, we cherished this moment of privacy.

Donald and I kept our secret as long as we could until it was impossible to hide any longer. On September 27, 2005, the *New York Post* broke the news: "Donald Trump is about to get a new apprentice."

Each woman's pregnancy experience is unique, and I consider myself fortunate to have enjoyed my time carrying my child.

While the first few months presented some challenges with morning sickness, that uncomfortable period seemed to pass by quickly. I have always been incredibly health-conscious and selective about what I eat. However, now that I was nurturing a new life within me, my standards reached new heights. I only ate the purest, preservative-free foods and completely cut out soda from my diet. It was a small sacrifice to ensure the best for my growing baby. I also incorporated regular Pilates and aerobic exercises in my schedule.

As a first-time mother, there is a natural sense of nervousness about the unknown, but I remained hopeful and focused on taking care of myself and my growing baby. You hope everything will go well with no complications. You take care of yourself as best you can and live your life, all while marveling at the miracle of carrying another life inside you. It was truly extraordinary to feel how beautifully the body knows what to do.

I embraced the beauty of pregnancy. My body was changing, and I welcomed this celebration of life itself. I was the creator of life, and I was so proud of it. I let go of any pressure to hide my body—I honored my new curves and cherished every part of the journey and all the miracles it brought.

During my third trimester, Anna Wintour at *Vogue* approached me with an exciting concept. She proposed featuring me, very pregnant, in the magazine to celebrate the beauty of pregnancy and motherhood. I fully resonated with the idea, feeling proud and comfortable in my changing body. At seven months pregnant, I flew to Palm Beach to shoot with Annie Leibovitz. It was a wonderful celebration of life and the miracle of creating a new one.

"I think it's very sexy for a woman to be pregnant," I told the readers of *Vogue*, making clear that I believe that a pregnant woman is very attractive.

Seeing the stunning photographs in the magazine the following April only confirmed my decision to celebrate pregnancy.

M

Stepping into a marriage with Donald, I found myself navigating the intricate dynamics of his big family. It demanded flexibility and openness, but each moment was a chance to connect, learn, and grow in this new environment.

By the time Donald and I married and welcomed Barron, his older children—Don Jr., Ivanka, and Eric—had become more independent, while Tiffany remained in her formative years, residing with her mother in California.

My approach to building relationships with Donald's children has always been grounded in love and respect. I recognize their individuality, understanding that, as their stepmother, my role is not to replace their mothers but to nurture a supportive and amicable connection. This perspective has enabled me to cultivate meaningful relationships with each child in a unique way.

While I may not agree with every opinion or choice expressed by Donald's grown children, nor do I align with all of Donald's decisions, I acknowledge that differing viewpoints are a natural aspect of human relationships.

It is essential to remember that each person is deserving of respect and understanding, regardless of disagreements. I have focused on creating an environment where everyone feels free to express themselves authentically. Rather than imposing my views or critiquing others, I have aimed to be a steady presence—someone they can rely on.

In any relationship, whether as a mother to my son, a wife to my husband, or a stepmother, I firmly believe in the principle:

Don't control, communicate!

I understand that being possessive is not conducive to a healthy family dynamic. Each member requires their own space, and I have made it a priority to respect that need.

This commitment has allowed me to remain true to myself, nurturing my independence while embracing my roles within the family. It has been vital for me to set boundaries and maintain my individuality, preparing myself to navigate the diverse challenges life presents.

When obstacles arise, I have learned to take responsibility for addressing them myself, rather than relying on others to resolve issues for me.

While we may share the same last name, each of us is distinct, with our own aspirations and paths to follow.

M

Barron William Trump came into this world in March 2006.

The experience of being a mother brought me a sense of warmth, love, purpose, and fulfillment that I had never felt before. Through this journey, I discovered my own strength, the incredible capabilities of a woman's body, and the instinctual drive to protect and care for another life. I learned how to adapt and prioritize my life, how to function on minimal sleep, and how to manage the inevitable exhaustion and anxieties that come with motherhood. The constant thoughts of my child's well-being, sleep patterns, and feeding habits were all new challenges that I faced with determination and love. The experience of motherhood has been a profound learning process, one that has shaped me in ways I never could have imagined.

I found myself cherishing the moments when I held Barron in my arms and gazed into his eyes. His presence brought me a sense of gratitude, appreciating his innocence and the love we shared. Watching Donald interact with Barron was heartwarming as well. His connection with his son showcased a different side of him that I had not seen before. Their relationship was filled with love and admiration, and it was truly touching to witness.

On weekdays, Donald was often occupied with work, leaving me as Barron's primary caregiver, and on weekends we would escape the city to Westchester, Bedminster, or Mar-a-Lago. It was there that Barron took his first swings at golf with Donald, first swimming lessons with my father, and tennis lessons with me. Despite the challenges of attracting attention on Fifth Avenue, our home provided a space where we could enjoy a normal family life. I made it a priority to create a nurturing and loving environment for Barron to thrive in.

When Barron entered the world, I deliberately chose to step back from public life. During those early years of Barron's life, my primary focus was providing him the care and attention he needed. While I still occasionally appeared at gatherings and events, my focus shifted to creating a sanctuary at home for my son. The allure of glamorous photo shoots and a jet-setting lifestyle no longer held sway over me, as my heart was captivated by the joy of nurturing and raising Barron. My career took a back seat to the most important role of all—being a devoted mother.

As a new mom, I was fortunate to be able to look to my own mother for guidance. My mother was a private yet deeply connected individual. She valued authentic connections and friendships, always steering clear of gossip and negativity, a principle I cherish in my own life. Now, as a mother, I strove to guide and support my child without imposing my will, just as she did with me. She believed in allowing others to carve their own paths, a philosophy I wholeheartedly embrace. Unlike many mothers of her time, she never pressured me to marry early or start a family before I was ready. She understood the importance of self-discovery and independence before entering into any partnership.

Her firm dedication to her daughters, and later to her cherished grandson, exemplified the virtues of patience and growth. Through her tender care and abundant love, she demonstrated that with time and nurturing, we can all flourish into our most radiant selves.

My mother's quiet strength and firm devotion to her family shaped me into the person I am today, and I strive to embody these qualities in my own life, knowing that her legacy lives on through me. My beloved mother was the richest thread in my life, weaving warmth, wisdom, and grace into every moment we shared.

There is an unparalleled sorrow in losing a mother, a profound heartache that shatters the spirit into fragments. For me, this heartache feels insurmountable, and the weight of grief is overwhelming.

On January 9th, 2024, as I bid her farewell, I was left with a profound sense of loss, yet an enduring gratitude for the unconditional love she bestowed upon me. Her beautiful spirit will forever illuminate my path. In her honor, I embrace her memory, cherishing the legacy of kindness and strength.

My eulogy read:

> My mother, the epitome of elegance and grace, exemplified the essence of a true woman. Her love for her husband Viktor—my father, Ines—my sister, and me was boundless. Her nurturing spirit had no limits, creating a legacy that will last for generations. She showered her grandson Barron with affection, illuminating his world with love, tender care, and unwavering devotion.
>
> In her presence, we were enveloped in the warmth of her embrace. We will be forever grateful for the unparalleled affection she bestowed on us. She embodied the best mother, wife, grandmother, mother-in-law—a true beacon of love and luxury in our lives.
>
> With her beauty and impeccable sense of style, she turned the heads of many. But it's not just her appearance that set her apart. It's her unwavering dedication and hard work that truly made her exceptional. Like a string that holds everything together, she balanced the demands of motherhood with grace and poise. From managing the household to pursuing her own ambition in fashion, she never ceased to amaze with her resilience and determination.
>
> Amalija is a name that carries significant meaning in various cultures, symbolizing qualities such as strength, dedication, and a strong work ethic. Her name was really a perfect match. She

worked tirelessly, pushing herself beyond her limits, fueled by the fire within. She is a true inspiration, a role model to me, and to so many.

With her passion for cooking, she transported every dish, which she curated with the spices from her garden, to new heights. For those who experienced her cooking creations, it was bliss. I am fortunate that she taught me many of her secrets to creating her signature delights.

Her experiences and sophistication were shared with me at a very young age and opened my eyes to the true essence of couture. She effortlessly introduced me to the charming world of fashion, with tales of her glamorous travels to Paris and neighboring European capitals.

With each whispered detail of the splendid fashion shows, spectacular cities, and chic boutiques, she ignited a passion within me, a desire to immerse myself in this extraordinary universe. Her travels became my gateway to the land of fashion allure, forever changing my perception of the art form, and inspiring me to embrace this captivating industry.

She was a creator of dreams, and I am forever grateful for the beauty she brought into my life. I will always cherish our time together. Often, in the late hours of the evenings, we sketched designs and made patterns together, and then, with each stitch, she finished crafting a masterpiece. Her hands always delicately weaved threads of opulence, every detail meticulously designed, and ultimately transformed into a piece of artwork.

Her sense of adventure opened a lens beyond Slovenia— unforgettable family ski trips in the Alps and idyllic summers spent on the breathtaking aquamarine shores of the Dalmatian coast. She adored the radiant sun, as its golden rays sun-kissed her skin as she strolled along the beautiful waters. In the following years, she often texted me gorgeous snapshots of Mother Nature's landscape.

She left the familiarity of her homeland to be with her newborn grandson in the United States. He was my mother's compass and focus.

With each step she took, she embraced the privilege bestowed upon her and, in time, the privilege of becoming a US Citizen. She vowed to contribute, to make a difference in a world filled with uncertainty. She exuded an exquisite sense of pride as my husband became the president of the United States, and as I embarked on a grand odyssey, traveling the corners of the globe as the First Lady.

My father, my sister, Barron, Donald, and I will forever remember the echoes of our laughter that we shared with our beloved Babi over fun dinners and travels. Her conversations flowed effortlessly, adorned with grace and charm. No topic was off-limits. In her presence, the world seemed to shimmer with radiant joy. She was not just a friend but a confidante, a beacon of light in the darkest of days.

In her company, I found peace, knowing that she would always be there to listen. She celebrated our successes and provided unwavering support during chaotic times. Our bond was unbreakable, a testament to the power of true love for one another.

She was my dear friend, an irreplaceable treasure, a gift bestowed upon me by the universe. And for that, I am eternally grateful.

Rest in peace, my beloved Mami.

M

It was only a few months after Barron was born that our family would mark another significant change—this one less public but still deeply meaningful. In July 2006, I became an American citizen. As I would recall in a speech at a naturalization ceremony at the National Archives seventeen years later:

> Throughout our lives, we cross thresholds. And although obstacles often stand in the way of our goals, we persevere, as we understand that conquering them will provide great access to personal development, fulfillment, and eventually self-actualization.
>
> For me, reaching the milestone of American citizenship marked the sunrise of certainty. At that exact moment, I forever discarded the layer of burden connected with whether I would be able to live in the United States. I hope you are blanketed with similar feelings of comfort right now. Finally, I could plan all of the aspects of my life. I recall feeling a tremendous sense of pride and belonging after I recited the United States Oath of Allegiance, as the pathway to citizenship is arduous.
>
> I was born and raised in the picturesque country of Slovenia, where my parents taught me the importance of a strong work ethic and pursuing my dreams. The values they instilled in me at an early age inspired my fashion and modeling career, and brought me to beautiful cities like Paris and Milan.
>
> While working internationally had its share of rules and regulations, it wasn't until I moved to New York City in 1996, that this system truly tested my determination. Upon my arrival, I immediately knew that I wanted to make the United States my permanent home. With the goal of securing a worker visa, I began researching, visiting consulates and embassies, and compiling the required records of my work experiences.
>
> Quickly, my life turned into a labyrinth of organizing paperwork. (Back then, the convenience of technology's document filing didn't really exist to the extent it does today.) Patience and perseverance became my constant companions as I navigated

through this intricate web, which I am sure you can all relate to. Even if very time-consuming, my dream of becoming a citizen pushed me to meticulously gather every last piece of information required, ensuring that no detail was overlooked.

My personal experience of traversing the challenges of the immigration process opened my eyes to the harsh realities people face (including you) who try to become US citizens. And then, of course, there are the nuances of understanding the United States immigration laws, and the complex legal language contained therein. I was very devoted, but I certainly was not an attorney, and eventually, it proved critical for me to retain counsel. I was fortunate to do so, as ultimately my journey was streamlined and brought me over the finish line, as a naturalized citizen.

While the challenges were numerous, the rewards were well worth the effort. I applaud you for every step you took, every obstacle you overcame, and every sacrifice you made. It's an honor to stand with you in these hallowed halls today in the presence of the Declaration of Independence. The very document on which our Founding Fathers carefully composed the words that capture the ideals surrounding individual liberty and this great republic. Arguably, one of the most important documents of all time.

Becoming an American citizen comes with responsibility. It means actively participating in the democratic process and guarding our freedom. It also means leading by example and contributing to our society. It is a life-altering experience that takes time, determination, and sometimes even tremendous strength.

You are now a part of a Nation with a rich history of progress, innovation, and resilience. Though you come from 25 different countries, your dreams and aspirations intertwine with those who have come before you, since 1776, and together, shape the future of this extraordinary country.

Be proud of yourself, stand your ground, and embrace the opportunities that lie ahead. You are American—be a beacon of inspiration for your children, and those who follow in your footsteps. May your journey continue to be filled with endless possibilities, and may your contributions enrich the fabric of this great Nation.

On the day of my swearing-in ceremony. Donald and I arrived at the courthouse together. The room was filled with diverse people from various backgrounds and cultures, speaking many different languages.

"Home," I reflected on my way back to Trump Tower that day, had meant so many things to me over the years: Sevnica, my little town by the Sava river; Ljubljana and the apartment I shared with my sister; Milan; Paris; the little one-bedroom in midtown Manhattan I'd found and furnished myself; and our family's residence at the top of Trump Tower. As I stated before, I had been a citizen of the world, and now, finally, I was also an American.

Chapter 6

All Business

By 2009, with Barron now in preschool, I was able to carve out some time for projects beyond motherhood. As I looked toward the future, I was excited for the new ventures and opportunities that would come my way. While I had considered expanding beyond modeling and tapping into my creativity, I had been selective in choosing career projects that aligned with my values.

Then, in 2009, Marc Beckman, Chief Executive Officer of the award-winning agency DMA United, presented me with the idea of creating a jewelry line, and the timing felt just right. My love for jewelry had been nurtured since childhood, flipping through the glossy magazines my mother brought home from her trips to Paris and other foreign cities. Given my love for art, design, and creativity, and having worked in the fashion industry for almost twenty years, the opportunity to design jewelry was thrilling and felt like a perfect new venture.

I started to develop a concept inspired by a beautiful gold bracelet my father had given to my mother. This symbol of love and family was later replicated for my sister and me, and it ultimately led me to the idea of creating a timeless and meaningful collection for a wider audience. Taking into account the questions so many women asked me about my personal jewelry choices, I began crafting pieces that reflected my own style and resonated with me on a personal level. I conceived the idea of three distinct collections, each inspired by a place that held significance to me: the Paris collection would be glamorous; the New York collection would be more business-oriented; and the Palm Beach collection would embody "sporty elegance."

Each collection was carefully curated to reflect the unique charm and character of its namesake city, while also ensuring that all items were priced at a reasonable level. By offering these collections for under $200, my goal was to make fashion more accessible. I wanted to empower women to treat themselves to something special, whether as a gift from a loved one or a well-deserved splurge for themselves.

Returning to design after so many years was a wonderful experience. Each creation was a labor of love, from a bold, braided chain necklace to a cocktail ring featuring an emerald-tinted stone and timepieces with stunning mother-of-pearl dials. I had been watching my mother design patterns as a child, which deepened my appreciation for the hard work that goes into creating a finished product. I was excited to share these new designs with the world.

QVC broadcasted the hour-long 8 o'clock segment on the first night, followed by another hour the next morning. The collection sold out within forty-five minutes, sparking a three-year success story. The demand for my designs only continued to grow over the next three years, with each appearance on the network resulting in record-breaking sales. Making multiple appearances on the network, I enjoyed engaging with viewers and providing style advice. Callers often complimented my style and jewelry: "It's so nice to talk to you. I love your style; I love your jewelry." I couldn't help but feel a sense of pride in knowing that I was contributing to making the world a more beautiful place, one stunning piece of jewelry at a time.

Financial independence is a core value of mine, and I have always been driven to work hard and earn my own money. Starting work at a young age myself and watching my parents work hard throughout their lives has instilled in me a strong work ethic and a desire for independence. I have never been one to sit idly by, even with the comfort of a successful husband by my side.

I firmly believe in the virtue of maintaining control over one's own life, regardless of whom you marry. Running my own business has given me such confidence, and I have always wanted to encourage women to pursue their passions and achieve success. Managing my jewelry company was about inspiring women to be independent as well as creating beautiful pieces. Melania Timepieces and Jewelry represented my passion, my project, and my business—a symbol of independence, self-respect, and empowerment for all women.

M

Throughout my teenage years, I made it a priority to care for my skin diligently. I invested time in researching and educating myself on the most beneficial products, gravitating toward natural options and avoiding harsh chemicals. As I embarked on my modeling career, I began experimenting with different skincare routines, often mixing products or creating my own. People frequently asked me about my regimen, marveling at the health of my skin.

In 2011, the CEO of New Sunshine, an Indiana-based company, approached me with the idea of creating a line of high-end skincare products. The concept seemed full of potential. Knowing I would commit wholeheartedly to any project, I wanted to ensure we developed the highest-quality products that would reach a broad consumer base. New Sunshine, run by successful businesspeople, seemed like the perfect match. It felt like the ideal next step in my journey.

After several months of contract negotiations, we finalized the agreement. Feeling optimistic about the partnership, we signed a five-year deal: I would create and promote the products, and New Sunshine would handle manufacturing and distribution.

I approached this venture with the same enthusiasm I had applied to my jewelry line, building it from the ground up. Meeting with chemists to learn about lotions, creams, and serums—understanding which ingredients would work harmoniously, which would spoil, and which might clash—became part of my weekly routine. With several major department stores on board, the products needed to be exceptional. Over the next few months, we developed several items: the Fluid Day Serum, the Luxe Night with Vitamins A and E, cleansing balm, and an exfoliating peel, all priced between $50 and $150. In my meetings with chemists, I discovered the rejuvenating properties of caviar, which led to the creation of formulas incorporating this unique ingredient.

Melania Caviar Complexe C6 went into production in 2013, with products set to hit stores that spring. I promoted the line through numerous TV and print interviews, including appearances on *Good Morning America* and *The View*. The response was overwhelmingly positive; people were genuinely interested. This collection, much like the jewelry line, was a source of immense pride for me. The products were superb, the packaging beautiful, and we had every indication that the line would sell well. The final step was ensuring that the products reached stores and were available on shelves.

The full rollout never materialized. The products were briefly available at Lord & Taylor before internal issues at New Sunshine halted everything. The products weren't delivered, stores had no inventory, and eager customers were left empty-handed. My disappointment quickly turned to anger. The issues had nothing to do with me. They stemmed from a dispute between the owners, which led to lawsuits. Amid their disagreement, my contract was questioned, and the distribution of my products stopped. They blamed me, with one party falsely claiming that the other had signed an unauthorized agreement with me. In fact, my contract had been thoroughly and extensively negotiated and meticulously crafted and agreed upon by all parties involved.

I was the face of the brand and the failure to deliver was a threat to my reputation and integrity. I was deeply disappointed and frustrated and decided to take legal action. I brought a lawsuit regarding the contract dispute. The fallout from this situation had a detrimental impact on both consumers and my personal brand. It was made clear in court that this was not how business should be conducted, and the judge ruled in my favor, confirming the validity of my contract and awarding me a contract agreed settlement. Overall, this experience taught me valuable lessons about the complexities of the business world and the importance of ensuring that all parties involved are committed to fulfilling their obligations.

I remain proud of the products we created and the effort I put into promoting them, and I hope to have the opportunity to bring excellent skincare products to market in the future under more favorable circumstances.

Chapter 7

It Is Official

June 16, 2015, marked yet another carefully planned and executed change in our lives, one that had been years in the making. It was well before 5 a.m. when my alarm went off. From our apartment high up in Trump Tower, I could see the first light of dawn beginning to brighten the eastern sky. Mentally organizing the tasks that lay ahead, I took a minute to gather myself. As the mother of a nine-year-old boy, early wakeups and full days were my norm. A typical Tuesday would have me out of bed at 6:00, waking Barron, making his breakfast, and spending a little time with him before driving him to school. But today was no ordinary Tuesday. This day was a clear demarcation in our lives, dividing everything into before and after, a day that would be etched in memory not just for our family, but for the American people as well.

Our instructions were to be ready and down in Donald's office on the twenty-sixth floor before 11:00. Donald's adult children and their families would join us there. I went to check on Barron for a moment before the day's events began to unfold. He was still asleep when I entered his room, and I didn't want to wake him just yet. I touched his face and kissed him, pondering what this new chapter in our lives would mean for him, for all of us. The media scrutiny, the intense public attention. But I reassured myself that I would be there for him, no matter what.

I made myself a strong espresso and savored a quiet final moment, aware that it would be one of the last in what promised to be an exceptionally busy—and incredibly exciting—day. It was time to wake Barron. As I dressed him in his little blue suit, I went over the plan: We'd go together to Dad's office, and then he would join the family in the lobby and wait for me and Dad to come down the escalator from the mezzanine. Dad would give a speech, and then it would be official.

Donald and I had discussed this next step at length and mapped out our plans, ensuring that the timing was right for both our careers and our family. I was prepared for anything. But at the same time, we were entering uncharted territory. In a few hours, the Trumps were getting into politics.

It was 10:40 when we arrived, and Donald's office was buzzing with an almost-tangible energy. I kissed Barron and told him I'd see him downstairs. He hugged his dad and then went to join his siblings in the lobby. Although I hadn't been involved in planning the announcement—those details were managed by Donald, his advisers, and his grown children—the idea was straightforward: Donald and I would descend the escalator, Ivanka would introduce her father, Donald would deliver a brief speech, and then we would all pose for photos onstage.

Just before 11:00, Donald and I took the elevator down to the mezzanine, where a large, wildly enthusiastic crowd had gathered to greet us. The entire lobby was filled with people, cheering loudly. The music was blaring, the atmosphere electric. As soon as the crowd saw us get out of the elevator, they erupted in applause. In that moment, I realized just how momentous the day would be, the culmination of years of contemplation, planning, and anticipation on Donald's part. It was clearly the beginning of something extraordinary. I felt it, and everyone in the room felt it too.

Donald approached the mezzanine railing and looked out over the crowd below. He waved and gave two thumbs up before guiding me with his left hand to the escalator. I stepped on in front of him, and down we went, into a world that was, in many ways, entirely new to us. Fashion, modeling, business, New York—those felt like home. But this was different. Though the escalator ride lasted only a few seconds, the images would be broadcast around the world nonstop for days and weeks: Donald and I descending the escalator, launching a political career in a way that no one had ever seen before. It was a significant moment—a historic moment—and I felt so very proud to be a part of it.

Donald and I walked from the bottom of the escalator to the stage. Finding Barron, I stood beside him while Donald made his way to the podium.

"Wow. Whoa. That is some group of people," he said. "So nice, thank you very much. That's really nice. Thank you. It's great to be at Trump Tower. It's great to be in a wonderful city, New York. And it's an honor to have everybody here. This is beyond anybody's expectations."

The crowd was ecstatic.

"Our country is in serious trouble. We don't have victories anymore," he said.

I had seen Donald in front of crowds and cameras before, and he was always great. But today, he seemed to function on an even higher level. He was focused, impassioned, and serious. I could tell he was speaking from the heart, communicating his vision to the crowd and the country.

"Our enemies are getting stronger and stronger, by the way, and we as a country are getting weaker."

He spoke plainly, with a frankness most politicians wouldn't even attempt. He outlined all the problems our country was facing: China and Mexico, wars in the Middle East, forgotten veterans, crumbling infrastructure, disappearing jobs, crooked politicians, self-interested lobbyists, Obamacare, and, more than anything, terrible leadership.

"Now," he said, "our country needs a truly great leader, and we need a truly great leader now. We need a leader who wrote *The Art of the Deal.* We need a leader who can bring back our jobs, can bring back our manufacturing, can bring back our military, can take care of our vets. Our vets have been abandoned. And we also need a cheerleader."

Donald was a great cheerleader. I'd seen it myself in everything he did. He loved this country and could no longer stand by and watch it fall apart. "We need somebody that can take the brand of the United States and make it great again. It's not great again. We need—we need somebody—we need somebody that literally will take this country and make it great again. We can do that." As the speech went on, the crowd grew increasingly enthralled. They were hanging on every word. It felt like, finally, someone was giving voice to so many of the things the American people had seen for themselves and never heard their politicians talk about. Finally, a politician who wasn't lying to them, who was telling them the truth, hard as it was to accept.

"So ladies and gentlemen . . . I am officially running . . . for president of the United States," he said to rapturous applause. "And we are going to make our country great again. It can happen. Our country has tremendous potential. We have tremendous people." In one speech, he spoke to what so many Americans who felt abandoned by Washington were thinking. Donald understood all of this, and he was articulating it beautifully.

For the forty-five minutes he spoke, he laid out his dream for voters. He didn't hold back. He didn't pull any punches. He wasn't underhanded or excessively calculating in the way politicians often are. He didn't just tell people what they wanted to hear. He told people what they needed to hear.

After he finished, the family stood for photos. When concluded, Barron and I returned to our apartment, in the quiet of our home, it took a moment for everything to sink in: the campaign was now real. I knew that our lives had irrevocably changed and that the journey ahead would not always be easy. But I love this country; I have loved it since the day I arrived. I understood that if our family was called upon to serve alongside Donald, it would be a profound honor—the honor of a lifetime.

I felt immense pride for my husband that day and took a moment to reflect with awe and gratitude on the journey we had traveled together since our first meeting in New York almost two decades earlier.

Chapter 8

Why Was the Speech Not Vetted?

Upon Donald's announcement of his candidacy, the campaign quickly accelerated into high gear. He was traveling and speaking to vast groups of supporters practically every day, all across the country.

By the end of 2015, the Republican presidential nomination appeared to be within reach, but the American voters had yet to decide. The journey ahead would not be easy, but we were prepared to face any challenges that came our way. In early February 2016, twelve Republicans, including Donald Trump, were still vying for the presidential nomination. By the end of the month, the field had narrowed to just five candidates. Through strong debate performances and victories in key states, Donald Trump secured the Republican nomination by the end of May. This historic achievement marked a significant shift in American politics and solidified his position as the party's President of the United States nominee.

As planning for the Republican National Convention began, I learned that I would be part of the program, and I embraced this opportunity wholeheartedly. I was filled with immense pride for Donald and his vision for our country, and I approached the opportunity to speak at the convention with a sense of duty and responsibility. I was honored to have the chance to share my thoughts and beliefs with the American people.

I felt excited, but also nervous, since I didn't have much time to get ready. After asking the campaign for a writer for a few weeks, they provided me with the first draft of the speech. While I appreciated the effort put into crafting it, I felt the remarks didn't capture my voice nor embody the message I wanted to convey. I wanted a speech that aligned with my goals, shared my unique message, and reflected my personality.

The American people already knew my husband well, but they didn't really know me at all. Their limited understanding of me was based on sensational headlines and gossip. I wanted to present myself authentically, to share my story and background.

My RNC speech was my opportunity to support my husband and to introduce myself on my terms, in my own voice. I planned to speak about my childhood, family, and journey to the United States. I wanted to convey messages of kindness, compassion, and service to one's country. Additionally, I wanted to share insights about the Donald I knew, the man I believed would make a great leader for our nation. I was filled with ideas and enthusiasm, eager to create a significant moment for my husband, the campaign, and the movement. I had never addressed such a large audience on such an important night, and I felt the weight of this responsibility.

As the convention loomed, Donald suggested I connect with Meredith McIver, a representative from the Trump Organization who was working with the campaign, to help craft my speech. I gave her a call. During my review of many speeches of previous First Ladies, Michelle's emphasis on the fundamental values of hard work, integrity, and kindness resonated deeply, reflecting the core principles that were instilled in me by my parents during my upbringing in Slovenia.

In my discussions with Meredith, I conveyed the significance of parents imparting these values to their children. I believe that by embodying these principles in our daily lives, we can work toward creating a more harmonious world for all.

While I relied on Meredith to help me with the speech and the campaign to review it, I was pleased with the final result. Understanding the importance of the occasion, I dedicated myself to practicing in the days leading up to the convention. The campaign advisers listened attentively and suggested a few word changes to enhance the message. I also rehearsed multiple times with the teleprompter, feeling confident in my delivery.

On July 18, 2016, when my husband introduced me as the "next First Lady," I stepped into the spotlight with a confident smile. The audience's energy was palpable, fueling my determination to make a positive impact with my speech.

"You have all been very kind to Donald and me, to our young son, Barron, and to our whole family," I began. "It's a very nice welcome, and we are excited to be with you at this historic convention, I'm so proud of your choice for president of the United States, my husband, Donald J. Trump!"

The audience erupted in applause at the mention of his name. They cheered once more as I expressed my deep love for my family and for America. Their enthusiasm grew as I shared the story of my journey to becoming a US citizen.

In my closing remarks, I expressed that if honored to serve as First Lady, I would "use that wonderful privilege to try to help people in our country who need it the most. One of the many causes dear to my heart is helping children and women. You judge a society by how it treats its citizens. We must do our best to ensure that every child can live in comfort and security with the best possible education." These words came from the depth of my heart, and I was thrilled to share them with millions of Americans.

I concluded by highlighting the values of kindness, love, and compassion that Donald and I would bring to the White House. "My husband is ready to lead this great nation," I said. "He's ready to fight every day to give our children the better future they deserve. Ladies and gentlemen, Donald J. Trump is ready to serve and lead this country as the next president of the United States!"

My sense of accomplishment on our flight back home swiftly turned to dismay and shock as news of a potential accusation of plagiarism reached our campaign. My initial reaction was one of disbelief, but upon closer examination, the undeniable similarities between the two speeches left me reeling. The weight of this realization hit me with a force I had never experienced before.

Looking back, I realized that I had relied too much on others in this crucial endeavor. I had no prior experience with the protocols and process of a national convention, and I assumed the professionals on the campaign would do whatever was necessary and appropriate for such an important speech. I trusted that any and all political and legal vetting had been taken care of, but I now realized that the campaign and the RNC had left me on my own.

"Why was the speech not vetted?" I asked Donald in frustration. He expressed disappointment and was unable to provide me with an answer. Vetting speeches is a standard practice to ensure accuracy, appropriateness, and alignment with the intended message. It is important to thoroughly review and verify all content before presenting it to avoid any potential issues.

The absence of a detailed review was a glaring oversight that now cast a shadow on my work. Discovering the team's failure to perform their duty filled me with a profound sense of betrayal. These were professionals, charged with ensuring the success of our campaign, yet they failed to implement even the most fundamental safeguard. This negligence left me feeling completely abandoned. I felt a deep sense of outrage and disappointment.

Following the incident, Meredith publicly apologized, mentioning an impromptu phone call during which I had shared passages from Michelle's speech as examples, which were mistakenly included in the draft. While this explanation was technically accurate, the damage was done.

From then on, I realized the importance of being intimately involved with every detail of my public life. No longer would I delegate specific tasks or trust others to ensure my reputation was protected. I would have to handle that on my own. This experience, while difficult, served as a crucial lesson in the realities of the political world.

The RNC speech controversy marked a dramatic escalation in my already fraught relationship with the media. Their relentless criticism, fueled by a palpable hostility, left no room for any attempt at explanation or nuance. My words, which articulated a hopeful vision for the nation, were overshadowed by a barrage of personal attacks.

The attacks reached a new low two weeks after the speech. Nude photos of me, taken and published twenty years earlier in France, were splashed across the cover of the *New York Post* under the disgusting headline "Menage à Trump." The photos had never been circulated in the United States. The magazine that had originally published them had ceased to exist long before these images were unearthed, and now they were being shared for the sole purpose of damaging Donald's campaign. Furthermore, the photographs, taken in late 1996 for the

French fashion magazine *Max*, were not a source of shame for me. My upbringing in Europe had fostered a different perspective on nudity, a more open and accepting attitude. We were accustomed to beaches where nudity was commonplace, a natural and uncontroversial aspect of life. Attitudes toward the female body in the United States were starkly different.

The female form was once revered and honored in Western culture. Historically, artists produced magnificent paintings and sculptures that exalted the beauty of the feminine figure. Nudity was a medium through which humanity was elevated and celebrated. This sentiment resonated deeply with me when I posed for *Vogue* during my pregnancy. I believed then, as I do now, that women should take pride in their bodies, not feel shame. During my modeling days, posing nude was commonplace and hardly scandalous. To me, those images were artistic and tasteful, fitting for a publication like *Max*, which showcased many renowned supermodels. Unfortunately, these photographs were now being exploited for profit. In 2016, the photographer who resold them boasted of his financial gain, having never compensated me for the original shoot that was done at my agent's advice.

Even more troubling, when the photographer was questioned about the timeline of these photographs, he suggested they were taken in 1995. This misinformation led to unfounded allegations that I had illegally worked in the United States, a claim propagated by the *New York Post*. Although the photographer later admitted his error, the damage was done—sensationalized lies about me spread worldwide, driven by a shameful pursuit of scandal and profit.

In the face of such exploitation and deceit, I had to relearn another harsh lesson: media and individuals will exploit others for their own profit and fame.

Around that same time, on August 20, the *Daily Mail* published an article sourced from a "journalist" in Slovenia, alleging that I had worked as an escort before meeting my husband. This unfounded rumor had circulated online for a few weeks, following baseless claims by a Maryland-based blogger, who also asserted that I had suffered a nervous breakdown during the campaign. No attempts were made to verify these claims; if they had done so, I would have vehemently denounced these absurd falsehoods.

The attacks had reached an unprecedented low. We are living in a dangerous time when it comes to journalism. Today, most journalists believe that their primary purpose is to create a narrative rather than report the facts. As a result, journalistic integrity has collapsed. I questioned journalistic ethics—how could they fabricate stories about me, leading people to believe such falsehoods?

So, I sued.

Engaging legal representation in both the UK and the United States, I pursued two lawsuits against the *Daily Mail* and one against the blogger. Eventually, all three cases concluded in my favor, with the *Daily Mail* issuing a formal apology and agreeing to pay damages, stating, "We accept that these allegations about Mrs. Trump are not true and we retract and withdraw them." Similarly, the blogger also apologized, admitting, "I had no legitimate factual basis to make these false statements and I fully retract them. I acknowledge that these false statements were very harmful and hurtful to Mrs. Trump and her family, and therefore I sincerely apologize to Mrs. Trump, her son, her husband, and her parents for making these false statements."

The point of my lawsuits wasn't the damages I eventually collected, but rather about holding individuals to a standard where lying is not acceptable. It was crucial to take a stand, even knowing the media's relentless nature. Their bias against Donald extended to me by association, driven by a vindictive attitude of "anything to harm them." While I had anticipated such challenges to some extent, the intensity still shocked me. That campaign year would set the tone for my future relationship with the media—they would never treat me fairly. They persisted in fabricating stories, undermining my efforts on behalf of children, and focusing on trivial matters. Though I entered politics with this awareness, experiencing their tactics firsthand only reinforced my resolve to stay above the fray. More than anything, I was concerned for my son, Barron. He was just a young boy, barely ten years old. I dreaded the prospect of media scrutiny toward him. Our first year in politics only solidified my determination to shield my son from such unwanted attention. I anticipated that if Donald were to win, the media's scrutiny, deceit, and mistreatment would only escalate.

Chapter 9

On My Way

In 1999, when asked what kind of First Lady I would be if Donald became president, I said I would be very traditional, like Jackie Kennedy. In today's world of constant social media and internet exposure, even someone as poised as Jackie Kennedy would struggle to maintain the same level of control over their image. When Donald's candidacy became a reality in 2015, I recognized that my role as First Lady would have to be unique and individual, living in an era of advanced technology that was not present fifty years ago. The ability to carefully curate and present a perfect image to the public, as Jackie did during the Kennedy era, is no longer feasible in our modern age of instant sharing and scrutiny. The idea of a flawless, almost mythical first family seems unattainable in today's world.

My vision for advocacy, tradition, support, and nurturing would guide me through the journey ahead. I was committed to upholding the dignity and gravity of the First Ladyship and serving the American people with strength and grace.

I was determined to remain authentic to myself. While I acknowledged the significance of tradition, I found myself in unprecedented times: a nation divided, a hostile media, and my unconventional status as the first foreign-born First Lady in centuries. The United States is my beloved home, though not my birthplace; English is not my native tongue. Our family is not a political dynasty; we hail from a different realm. These differences compelled me to forge my own path, guided by my own principles and convictions.

I realized that not everyone would welcome me with open arms. The political landscape had already caused rifts in friendships. Seeing lifelong companions drift away after Donald's nomination was disheartening, but I knew it was all part of a political process. It became clear that surrounding myself with genuine, encouraging, and innovative individuals was essential—there was no room for negativity and drama in my world.

Regardless of political affiliations, I sought to pave the way for collaboration with individuals of all backgrounds, whether Democrat or Republican, who share a true dedication to the betterment of our nation. Embracing Donald's message of unity, I aimed to mend the divides that have plagued us. My loyalty was to every single American, regardless of their beliefs. I was committed to serving all individuals with fairness, respect, and integrity, upholding the values of our diverse society.

M

The morning after the election, the wheels of transition were already turning. Suddenly, my life was governed by the relentless whirlwind of a schedule that I had little control over. The itinerary for the week allowed no breaks, no flexibility or spontaneity. By Thursday—a mere two days after the election—we would depart for Washington to begin our inaugural duties as president and First Lady–elect. Our circle of acquaintances in D.C. was sparse—limited to a handful of New York politicians Donald had long engaged with and a few from his campaign days. It was time for Washington to get to know us.

Meanwhile, the phone rang incessantly. It felt like a dizzying task to navigate the ceaseless flood of calls and prepare for the imminent journey to D.C. and back. I recall a good friend calling me that day to extend her congratulations. "I'm so proud of you and Donald," she said. "It's amazing. Now, the whole world is on your shoulders." *Thanks!* I thought. But at least someone understood how I felt. Donald and I had been surrounded by throngs of people—supporters, advisers, security—for what seemed like weeks at that point, and the past twenty-four hours had been nonstop activity. When we finally returned home on election night, the hour was so late and my exhaustion so profound that any deep discussion about the momentous events—or our suddenly transformed future—seemed beyond reach.

Before everything *really* started up again, as Donald prepared to go down to his office on Wednesday morning, he and I had a private moment.

"Congratulations," I said. "What an achievement. All those other people . . . and *you* won. You're the president of the United States of America."

"And you're the First Lady," he said. "Good luck." I looked at him, momentarily unsure of his meaning. Good luck? I realized he wasn't worried, he was proudly confident I could handle the future. It was his unique way of saying, "Good luck—I know you'll excel. Let's get started."

Donald had always placed a considerable amount of trust in me—as a wife, mother, confidante, and adviser. That morning his trust felt particularly tender and profound, resonating with love and understanding of our future together. I was grateful for that moment before we would inevitably be pulled in myriad directions once more.

The next day, a Secret Service motorcade whisked us from Trump Tower to LaGuardia Airport, where we boarded Donald's 757 and prepared for takeoff. I was sleep-deprived, yet buzzing with anticipation; it felt as though the world around us was moving on fast-forward. When I settled into my seat, it took a minute to grasp what I saw on the TV screen in front of me: our plane getting doused with water as if in response to a fire emergency. There was no fire, and typically, ground crews didn't spray down the plane after passengers had boarded. Perplexed, I glanced out the window and spotted the source: two imposing yellow fire trucks positioned at a four-way junction on the tarmac, each sending arcs of water cascading over the plane as it taxied beneath. It dawned on me—it was a salute, a ceremonial gesture, a send-off filled with congratulations and good wishes. As we taxied toward the runway, I could see airport employees cheering and waving vigorously, honking their horns and flashing their lights. It served as a poignant reminder: our journey to Washington wasn't just our personal transition; the victory belonged to the entire nation. It was a beautiful moment—the first of many that day.

Our first destination in Washington was the White House, a place I had never visited before. Although it would grow familiar in the weeks and months ahead, everything felt new to me that morning. We entered through the South Lawn, where the Obamas greeted us and guided us into the house through the South Portico. The White House is an iconic structure, one that everyone can picture in their minds, yet I was struck by its enduring elegance. Traditional and venerable, yet undeniably sophisticated, it evoked a sense of gratitude in me to be entrusted with the responsibility of caring for it—one of the primary duties of the First Lady.

The four of us proceeded to the Oval Office, and Michelle graciously offered me a tour of the residence. We began with tea in the

Yellow Oval Room, exchanging thoughts about life in the White House. She was quick to answer my questions, and generous with her advice. Having been through a similar experience when Barack assumed the presidency when her daughters were young, she understood better than almost anyone else what lay ahead for Barron and me. Despite media expectations of awkwardness or tension, our meeting was cordial and pleasant.

Upon my return from Washington, my attention turned to the transition process and the formation of my team. An experienced Republican operative from the RNC who came prepared with a thorough agenda outlining our tasks, key roles to be filled, and potential candidates for consideration was instrumental in guiding me through this process. She came prepared with a thorough agenda outlining our tasks, key roles to be filled, and potential candidates for consideration.

One of the first things she presented to me was a poster-sized organizational chart of the First Lady's office, listing twenty-three distinct positions: chief of staff, deputy chief of staff, assistant to the deputy chief of staff. Assistant to the assistant.

Hiring these important roles felt like stepping into the leadership of a prestigious corporation despite a lack of industry knowledge. However, this wasn't a mere business venture—these were critical positions serving our nation with the utmost importance.

As a political newcomer, I faced the challenge of building my team from scratch. I understood the importance of finding qualified individuals, earning trust, and fostering effective teamwork. I took this responsibility very seriously.

Recognizing Donald's significant challenge in assembling his own team, I refrained from seeking his guidance or complaining about the workload. Donald allowed me to independently recruit and build my own team. I focused on the process and on assembling a team that would serve the nation effectively.

In addition to addressing staffing needs, I had a list of ideas, priorities, and initiatives I planned to explore as First Lady. My primary focus would be cybersecurity and the well-being of children—issues that I had long been passionate about and hoped to advocate for using my new platform. Along with this, I was also working on orchestrating the move from New York to Washington and preparing for the upcoming inauguration, both of which required my immediate attention. Drawing from experience, I knew being thoroughly organized was vital to success. In addition to my existing responsibilities, I managed to balance my duties for Barron—overseeing his meals, well-being, school activities, and transportation while diving into meetings, interviews, and crucial phone calls. This allowed me to be prepared as the inauguration date loomed closer. Naturally, I was concerned about the challenges that Barron might face during the upcoming transition. He needed to have faith that certain constants would remain unchanged despite the changes that lay ahead. Specifically, he needed to understand that his father and I would always be there to provide him with love and support and to safeguard him unconditionally.

I found myself eagerly anticipating the opportunities that lay ahead. Confident in balancing many roles, I refused to confine myself to compartments and aspired to serve as a beacon of inspiration for other women.

Chapter 10

My Husband, the President

On the morning of January 19, we arrived at Joint Base Andrews in Maryland aboard an Air Force 757—our final flight as president and First Lady–elect. A waiting motorcade took us to the capital, where, by constitutional mandate, the following day at noon would mark the official beginning of Donald's presidency and my tenure as First Lady. The city hummed with anticipation as supporters streamed in to join the celebration.

Donald headed off to a leadership luncheon, while Barron and I went to Blair House—the President's Guest House— where tradition dictates that our entire family would lodge for the night. This immaculate 70,000-square-foot mansion has been a sanctuary for visiting dignitaries since the 1940s. While Donald aimed to disrupt certain Washington conventions, we held a deep reverence for presidential traditions, such as our stay at Blair House. It was a privilege to uphold these customs.

Our day was filled with ceremonial duties. I stood by my husband's side and held his hand during a solemn wreath-laying ceremony at Arlington National Cemetery to honor our veterans.

As the sun began to set, Donald and I descended the grand steps of the Lincoln Memorial. Each step reminded me of the liberty and opportunity that this magnificent country bestows upon us. As Donald stood before the majestic Lincoln statue, a sea of people gazed up at him with anticipation. His commanding presence inspired confidence and authority as he began to address the crowd: "I'll see you tomorrow. And you're going to cheer me on but I'm going to be cheering you on because what we've done is so special." His voice carried across the square, inspiring the crowd with his words of promise and inspiration.

When my alarm chimed on January 20th, I noticed that the sun had not risen yet. The morning at Blair House was a whirlwind of activity, as our family prepared for the long day ahead. The rooms were assigned beforehand—Donald and me, Barron, my mother and father, all of Donald's children, their spouses, and the grandchildren. Every room was filled with excitement as we readied ourselves for the festivities. As I arrived at the glam room after a boost from a strong espresso and a light breakfast of fruit, my trusted team of Nicole, Mordachai, and Hervé was already gathered and ready to work.

There had been a lot of speculation about my outfit. I knew all eyes would be on me as I stepped out on this historic day. This dress was going to be captured in photos that would be recorded in history. I had chosen a stunning blue ensemble designed for me by the great American fashion designer Ralph Lauren—a mock turtleneck dress with a matching cashmere jacket and long blue gloves. My high-heeled Manolo Blahnik pumps matched the light blue color of the outfit.

The inauguration was a whirlwind of encounters and handshakes, making it a challenge to recall every precise detail. The day began with a prayer service at St. John's Episcopal Church, known as the "Church of the Presidents," a long-standing tradition spanning nine decades. Following this, we were chauffeured in the presidential limousine, known as "the Beast," to the White House, where we were greeted by the Obamas on the front steps. Barack congratulated Donald, and I presented Michelle with a robin's-egg blue Tiffany & Co. box, containing a silver picture frame. This gesture was a nod to tradition, as she had gifted Laura Bush a pen and journal on a previous occasion. We posed for photographs before enjoying a brief reception inside the White House. As we departed for the inauguration ceremony, Donald and Barack rode in the presidential Beast, while Michelle and I followed in a second limousine. Our conversation during the ride was pleasant and lighthearted.

Once we arrived at the Capitol, a marine in full-dress regalia guided me onto the inaugural platform, where Barron and my beloved mother and father eagerly awaited.

As I gazed out at the vast sea of distinguished individuals, surrounded by thousands of people, I felt a surge of pride and gratitude while also acknowledging the weight of the moment. As Chief Justice John Roberts prepared to swear in Donald as the president, I stood next to my husband, holding two historic Bibles: one given to Donald by his mother when he was a boy, and the other used by President Abraham Lincoln at his first inauguration. I knew this moment would be in my memory forever. "Please raise your right hand and repeat after me," Justice Roberts said.

Donald raised his right hand, placing his left on the Bibles. "I, Donald John Trump, do solemnly swear . . ."

"I, Donald John Trump, do solemnly swear . . ."

". . . that I will faithfully execute . . . the office of president of the United States . . . and will to the best of my ability . . . preserve, protect and defend . . . the Constitution of the United States." Donald repeated each phrase.

"So help me, God," the chief justice said.

"So help me, God," Donald affirmed.

"Congratulations," Justice Roberts said, shaking Donald's hand. My husband embraced me as the band struck up "Hail to the Chief."

My husband, the president.

Following the speech, there was a benediction; a stirring national anthem performance, and a ride to the east side of the Capitol for the outgoing president's departure ceremony. We bid farewell to the former president and First Lady beside the military helicopter that would take them to Joint Base Andrews, waving as they flew away. Next, we had lunch in the Capitol's National Statuary Hall, where Donald asked everyone to give Hillary Clinton a standing ovation—a commendable gesture of bipartisanship on his part.

The parade was a grand display, with eight thousand participants including bands, veterans' groups, and military units marching alongside us. The sight was truly impressive. While we mostly rode in the armored limo, we followed tradition by stepping out twice to walk up Pennsylvania Avenue and engage with the enthusiastic crowd.

After arriving at the White House in the late afternoon, we proceeded to prepare for the evening's festivities, which comprised three inaugural balls: the Liberty Ball, the Freedom Ball, and the Salute to Our Armed Services Ball. I then changed into my evening gown for the occasion.

In the weeks leading up to the inauguration, I had found myself in a whirlwind of events, realizing I had perhaps waited a bit too long to secure the perfect gown. Then a dear friend from Belgium who lives in Paris, Régine Mahaux, told me I needed to meet the talented Hervé Pierre.

Hervé has an impressive background, having worked with haute couture fashion houses such as Christian Dior and Pierre Balmain as well as Oscar de la Renta and Caroline Herrera. His portfolio spoke volumes about his talent and expertise.

After our first meeting on January 3, I was convinced that we were destined to create something stunning for the upcoming inaugural ball. We discussed my vision for a unique off-white, off-the-shoulder gown. The timeline was tight, but Hervé was unfazed and eager to collaborate. We brainstormed ideas and he quickly got to work on sketches. After several iterations, we settled on a design that was both modern and elegant: a sleeveless vanilla-colored gown with a distinctive arch across the torso, a high slit, and a striking red silk belt. Hervé's attention to detail and creative flair truly brought my vision to life, and I was thrilled with the final result.

Hervé personally greeted me at the White House following the inaugural parade to ensure the dress was flawless. It was indeed perfect, and I was fully prepared for the ball.

In my couture gown, I danced with my husband to the timeless melody of Frank Sinatra's iconic "My Way" at the Liberty Ball and the Freedom Ball. Our evening ended at the National Building Museum for the Salute to Our Armed Services Ball. Surrounded by distinguished military personnel, we connected with the brave soldiers at Bagram Airfield in Afghanistan via satellite. As we expressed our gratitude for their valiant service, and they cheered us on, I felt immense pride knowing that Donald not only held the title of president of the United States, but also served as the commander in chief of the entire US military.

As Donald and I stepped into our new home—the White House—very late, the chief usher guided us through the corridors and into the residence, where I immediately kicked off my high-heeled stilettos. I realized the importance of a good night's rest. Tomorrow's schedule promised to be just as demanding as today's. Truthfully, the

White House felt more like a hotel than a home that first night. The Obamas had just moved out, and our entire family was staying through the weekend.

Sleeping in the White House that first night, amid many unforgettable experiences, seemed like a perfect way to end the day—almost too remarkable to believe.

On Saturday, January 21, Donald and I attended the National Prayer Service at the Washington National Cathedral. Later in the evening, the whole family gathered for a dinner in the State Dining Room. My parents, along with all of Donald's children and grandchildren, were present. The next day, January 22, marked our twelfth wedding anniversary. So much had happened in those twelve years, and it felt right to celebrate everything at once—the inauguration, my husband as the president, our marriage, our new home, and our new lives. This was the beginning of a new adventure, and we were thrilled to embark on it together. My husband's inauguration marked a profound moment in our lives and the country's history. While tradition dictated much of the ceremony, those in D.C. would agree that Donald's inauguration felt different—charged with new energy. Enthusiastic crowds of supporters surrounded us, people who had traveled from across the country to celebrate with us. Their excitement was palpable.

Chapter 11

In the White House

When Donald won the Republican nomination, someone remarked to me that being First Lady is often referred to as the "hardest volunteer job in America." It is a role that is undefined, unpaid, highly visible, and subject to relentless scrutiny. However, I believe that it also presents power and ample opportunities for making a positive impact. Previous First Ladies have shown that we have the power to effect significant change, and I was committed to using my platform for the greater good.

The role of the First Lady encompasses a wide range of responsibilities. Beyond family duties, the First Lady oversees approximately one hundred White House staff, including housekeepers, plumbers, engineers, chefs, florists, and carpenters. She plans and hosts all annual White House events, such as the Easter Egg Roll, Thanksgiving and Christmas gatherings, and visits from foreign dignitaries. She often travels with the president, which involves meticulous planning between the First Lady's and the West Wing staff. Additionally, the Office of the First Lady manages her own schedule, initiatives, and travel. There are also unforeseen events—national tragedies, natural

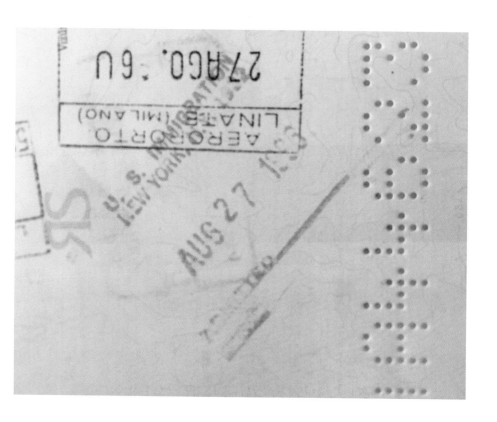

A page of my passport, stamped
at JFK airport when I first arrived
in America, NYC, August 27, 1996

posite top: Addressing delegates on the
st day of the Republican National Convention,
veland, Ohio, July 2016

posite middle left: Speaking at a rally,
ain Line Sports Center, Berwyn, Pennsylvania,
vember 2016

posite middle right: With Donald before he
dresses his supporters, Milwaukee, Wisconsin,
bruary 2016

posite bottom left: At the Presidential Debate
h Hofstra University, Hempstead, New York,
ptember 2016

posite bottom right: On the campaign trail,
rtle Beach, South Carolina, November 2015

o: My husband, the president-elect, Trump Tower,
C, November 8, 2016

ttom: On stage, election night, NYC,
vember 8, 2016

Top left: Amalija Ulčnik and Viktor Knavs, my
parents, on their wedding day in 1967

Top right: My maternal grandparents Amalija and
Anton Ulčnik, on their wedding day in 1935

Bottom left: My mother in Slovenia, 1965

Bottom right: My father in Slovenia, 1960

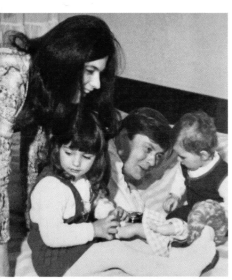

Top: My parents, Ines, and I on my first birthday,
April 26, 1971

Bottom, left and right: My family, Slovenia,
1971 and 1973

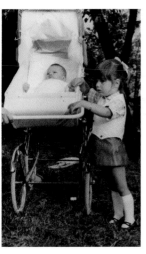
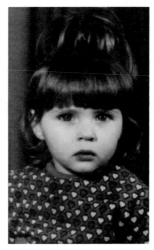

Top left: My mother, Amalija, 1970
Top right: My father, Viktor, 1970
Bottom left: Ines and I, 1970
Bottom center and right: Me, 1973

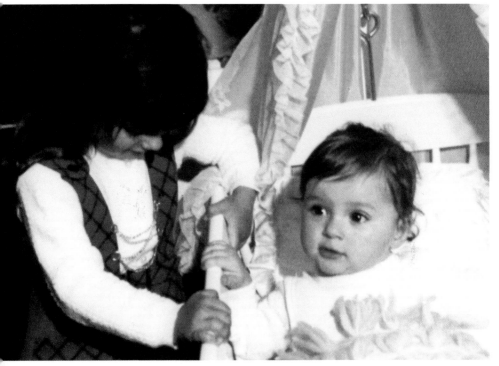

Top: Ines and I, 1971

Bottom left: My first birthday, April 26, 1971

Bottom right: With my mother, celebrating my
3rd birthday, April 26, 1973

Top: In the countryside with my mother and Ines, 1971

Bottom: Ines and I, 1971

Opposite top left: Me at home, 19[

Opposite top right: Ines and I, 19[

Opposite bottom: My father's Citroën Maserati SM, 1977

Opposite top:
Dalmatian Coast with my
parents, Croatia, 1982

Opposite bottom left:
Dalmatian Coast, summer 1983

Opposite top right:
My mother, Croatia, 1984

Opposite bottom right:
Water-skiing with my father,
Dalmatian Coast, Croatia, 1980

Top (center) and bottom (right):
My first time as a model on the
runway, 1976

osite: My first modeling photos,
ljana, Slovenia, 1997

A photo of me taken by Ines,
natian Coast, 1984

om left: My sister Ines, Slovenia, 1995

om right: My favorite of Ines's
tings, Slovenia, 1992

Top: Portfolio image, Milan, 1992

Bottom: My award for winning the
Cinecittà Cinematographic International
contest, Rome, 1990

RICCARDO GAY

M O D E L ■ M A N A G E M E N T

VIA REVERE ■ 20123 MILANO-ITALY

NT 48 00 27 13 - T.V. 48 13 273 FAX 48 00 55 08 - STAGE 48 00 27 75 FAX 48 00 85 77

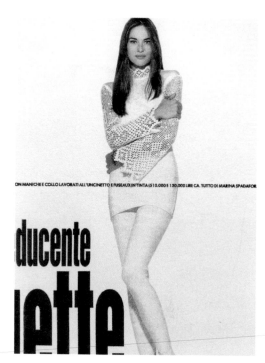

ON MANICHE E COLLO LAVORATI ALL'UNCINETTO E FUSEAUX IN TINTA L510.000 $ 130.000 LIRE CA. TUTTO DI MARINA SPADAFOR

ducente

lette

MELANIA

Altezza 1,77 Seno 88 Vita 59 Fianchi 90 Scarpe 40 Occhi blu Capelli castani
Height 5'9½ Bust 34½ Waist 23½ Hips 35½ Shoes 10 Eyes blue Hair brown

UTO ELASTICIZZATO CON BOTTONCINI SUI POLSI (INES DE LA FRESSANGE, 2.

silhouette

Top left: My modeling card at Riccardo
Gay Model Management in Milan, 1993

Top right and bottom left, right: Editorial
work, Italy, 1993

Top left:
Editorial image, Paris, 1993

Top right:
Editorial image, NYC, 1997

Bottom:
Editorial image, France, 1995

Opposite top left, right:
Editorial images, NYC, 1997

Opposite bottom left:
Sports Illustrated, Swimsuit
Issue, 2000

Opposite bottom right:
The Camel ad campaign, Time
Square, NYC, 1997

Top: Donald and I on our first date
night in NYC, September 1998

Opposite, top left: At the MoMa Film
Benefit Gala, NYC, 2008

Opposite, top right: "The Donald"
Friars Club Roast, NYC, 2004

Bottom left: At *Time Magazine*'s 100 Most Influential People Celebration, NYC, 2005

Bottom right: With Donald at the New York special screening of *The September Issue*, 2009

Top left: At home, NYC, 2002

Top right: Costume Institute Gala at The Metropolitan
Museum of Art, NYC, 2004

Bottom left: At Mar-a-Lago, 2005

Bottom right: Golden Globes, Los Angeles, California, 2007

left: Donald and I exchanging vows, The Church of Bethesda-By-The Sea,
m Beach, January 22, 2005

right: As newlyweds, The Church of Bethesda-By-The Sea, Palm Beach, 2005

ttom left: Interior of Mar-a-Lago ballroom, January 22, 2005

ttom right: After-party on my wedding night, Mar-a-Lago, Palm Beach, 2005

VOGUE

FEB

Opposite, top: *Vogue*, 2005

Opposite, bottom, left to right: With John Galliano, Manolo Blahnik, Olivier Theyskens, Paris, 2004

Top: In the Dior showroom, Paris, 2004

Bottom, left to right: Valentino, NYC, 2004
Nicolas Ghesquiere, Karl Lagerfeld, Paris, 2004

At home with Barron, March 2006

Annie Leibovitz for *Vogue*, Palm Beach, 2006

Celebrating Barron's 1st birthday,
Mar-a-Lago, 2007

Celebrating Barron's baptism,
Mar-a-Lago, December 2006

Top left: Barron and I in Palm
Beach, 2009

Top right: My parents and
Barron, Bedminster, 2006

Bottom left: Donald and Barron,
traveling from New York to Palm
Beach, 2006

Bottom right: Barron with
my mother and father, Palm
Beach, 2009

Top left: With my parents and Barron, Palm Beach, 2009

Top right: My mother and Barron, Palm Beach, 2009

Bottom: With my mother, Palm Beach, 2015

Top: Barron with his siblings, Donald Jr., Ivanka, Eric, and Tiffany, NYC, January 2014

Bottom: Barron with his father, NYC, January 2016

Barron and I at home, NYC,
uary 2016

om: Barron and I,
-a-Lago, March 2011

Opposite top:
Barron and I at home in my
office, NYC, 2010

Opposite bottom, left and right:
On the set at QVC Studios, 2010

Opposite bottom center:
Melania Timepieces & Jewelry
Collection, 2010

Top:
Wearing jewelry and a timepiece
from my collection, 2010

Bottom left:
Caviar Complexe C6 skincare
line, 2013

Bottom right:
Campaign ad for my Caviar
Complexe C6 skin care line, 2013

Caviar Complexe C6™

Preliminary organization structure for the Office of the First Lady

```
                                          AP & Chief of
                                          Staff to the First
                                          Lady
┌ ─ ─ ─ ─ ─ ─┐  ┌──────────────┐                              ┌──────────────┐ ┌──────────────┐
│Exec. Residence│ │Personal Aide to│                          │Senior Adviser│ │WH Visitor's Office│
│ Chief Usher  │  │    FLOTUS    │                             │              │ │   Director   │
│  FL Maid     │  │              │                             └──────────────┘ └──────────────┘
│Career Staff  │  └──────────────┘
└ ─ ─ ─ ─ ─ ─┘
                        ┌──────────────┐
                        │SAP & Deputy Chief│
                        │   of Staff   │
                        └──────────────┘
                        ┌──────────────┐
                        │Assistant Chief of│
                        │    Staff     │
                        └──────────────┘
```

Executive Assistant to the Chief of Staff	SAP & Director of Policy and Projects	SAP & Director of Communications	SAP & Social Secretary	Director of Scheduling & Advance	Director of Correspondence
	Deputy Director of Policy and Projects	Press Secretary	Deputy Social Secretary	Dep. Director of Advance / Trip Director	Associate Director of Correspondence
		Deputy Press Secretary	Deputy Social Secretary	Dep. Director of Scheduling / Events Coordinator	
		Staff Assistant / Speechwriter	Associate Social Secretary	Special Assistant / Travel Aide	*Volunteers*

Top: The organizational chart for t[...]
First Lady's office, November 2016

Bottom: In Bedford, New York, 201[...]

Opposite: *Harper's Bazaar* editoria[...]
NYC, 2016

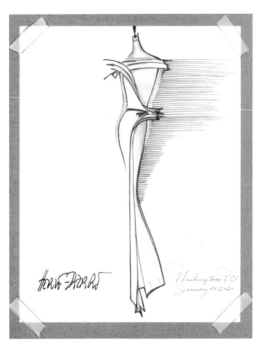

Top left: Hervé Pierre's sketch of my inaugural dress, January 2017

Top right: At the Liberty Ball in Washington, DC, Inauguration night, January 20, 2017

Bottom: The swearing-in ceremony at the U.S. Capitol, January 20, 2017

Opposite, top: Donald being sworn in as president, U.S. Capitol, January 20, 2017

Opposite, bottom: Donald and I at the Inaugural Ball, January 20, 2017

Top: On Marine One, October 2020

Opposite top: On the First Lady's plane, November 2020

Bottom: In the presidential limousine, "The Beast," November 2020

posite top: The exterior of the tennis pavilion under construction, July 2020

posite middle left: With interior designer Tham Kannalikham and construction
nager Peggy Hogan at the construction site of the White House tennis pavilion, 2020

posite bottom left: The interior of the tennis pavilion while under construction, 2020

posite bottom right: The completed interior of the tennis pavilion, 2020

o: The newly built White House tennis pavilion, November 2020

ttom: Ribbon-cutting ceremony of the tennis pavillion, November 2020

Top: Looking over the plans for the White House Rose Garden with landscape architect Perry Guillot and project manager Ryan Busch, July 2020

Middle: The Rose Garden under construction, August 2020

Bottom left: The blooming Rose Garden, Spring 2021

Bottom right: Unveiling Isamu Noguchi's "Floor Frame" sculpture, Rose Garden, 2020

Top: Preservation and renovation of the White House private dining room, July 2018

Bottom left: The Queen's Bathroom under renovation, July 2018

Bottom right: The newly decorated Queen's Room

Top: At the newly renovated Camp David, January 2021

Middle left: The redesigned Yellow Oval Room, White House residence, December 2020

Middle right: The carpet designed by me, Yellow Oval Room, December 2020

Bottom left: The carpet designed by me, Diplomatic Reception Room, 2020

Bottom right: The newly designed and renovated White House bowling alley, April 2019

: Australia state dinner, Rose Garden, September 20, 2019

tom: Putting the final touches for the French state dinner, State
ng Room, April 24, 2018

Top: Greeting our guests at a White House
Christmas party, December 2020

Bottom: Receiving the White House Christmas tree,
November 23, 2020

ry Christmas, White House, 2020

Top: Donald signing a proclamation for "National Be Best Day," Rose Garden, White House, May 7, 2018

Bottom: Announcement day of my Be Best initiative, Oval Office, May 7, 2018

left: Visiting Neonatal Abstinence Syndrome
AS) patients at Thomas Jefferson University
spital, Philadelphia, October 2018

right: Highlighting some of the nation's most
asured National Parks and sharing Be Best's
ssage of wellbeing, Wyoming, October 2019

ddle left: Visiting the Microsoft Innovation and
icy Center, Washington, DC, July 2018

Middle right: Ringing the opening bell at the New
York Stock Exchange in connection with my Be Best
anti-bullying initiative. NYC, September 2019

Bottom left: Visiting the Mori Building Digital Art
Museum with Akie Abe in Tokyo, May 2019

Bottom right: Donald and I receiving an opioid
briefing by senior administration officials, Oval
Office, White House, March 2019

Top: Saudi King Salman bin Abdulaziz Al-Saud greeting us our arrival, Riyadh, Saudi Arabia, May 2017

Middle: At the meeting with King Salman bin Abdulaziz Al-Saud, Riyadh, Saudi Arabia, May 2017

Bottom: At the Western Wall, Jerusalem, Israel, May 2017

Opposite top: Meeting Pope Francis, Vatican City, May 2017

Opposite left: Donald and I at the Sistine Chapel, Vatican City, May 2017

Opposite middle right: With patients at Queen Fabiola Children's Hospital, Brussels, Belgium, May 2017

Opposite bottom: Visiting young patients at the Pediatric Hospital Bambino Gesù, Rome, May 2017

Top: At the Door of No Return, Cape Coast Castle, Ghana, October 2018

Center: Visiting children at the Greater Accra Regional Hospital, Accra, Ghana, October 2018

Bottom: Singing with children during my visit to the Nest Children Home orphanage, Nairobi, Kenya, October 2018

Top: Visiting Chipala Primary School, Lilongwe, Malawi, October 2018

Middle: At the David Sheldrick Elephant Orphanage, Nairobi, Kenya, October 2018

Bottom: At the Great Sphinx of Giza, Egypt, October 2018

Opposite top: Boarding Air Force One to visit our troops in Iraq for Christmas, December 25, 2018

Opposite bottom: With members of the military, Al Asad Air Base, Iraq, December 26, 2018

Top: Observing flight operations on the USS George H. W. Bush, December 2018

Bottom left: In the Osprey aircraft on my way to visit service members on the USS George H. W. Bush aircraft carrier, December 2018

Bottom right: Visiting service members and their families at Langley Air Force Base, Hampton, Virginia, December 2018

posite top: Akie Abe and I show
r calligraphy, reading "Peace,"
ring a visit to Kyobashi Tsukiji
mentary School, Tokyo, Japan,
vember 2017

posite bottom: With Chinese
esident Xi Jinping, his wife Peng
uan, and performers, after a
king Opera performance at the
lace Museum, Forbidden City,
ijing, China, November 2017

left: With Her Majesty Queen
zabeth II, Windsor Castle, UK,
ne 2018

right: At the Ceremonial
elcome with the Queen and the
chess of Cornwall, Buckingham
lace, UK, June 2019

ttom: Donald and I with Prince
arles, Prince of Wales, and his
e, Camilla, Duchess of Cornwall,
nfield House, UK, June 2019

Opposite top:
Briefing the governors on the the wellbeing of our nation's children, Situation Room, White House, May 18, 2020

Opposite bottom:
At a briefing with health officials on COVID-19, Oval Office, White House, February 2020

Top:
Visiting the Taj Mahal, Agra, India, February 2020

Bottom:
At Sarvodaya Co-Educational Senior Secondary School, New Delhi, India, February 2020

Opposite top: With local law enforcement personnel after visiting the Health and Human Services Southwest Key Campbell children's shelter, Phoenix, Arizona, June 2018

Opposite middle: Supporting communities damaged by Hurricane Michael, Lynn Haven, Florida, October 2018

Opposite bottom: Visiting with victims and first responders of the Las Vegas mass shooting, University Medical Center, Las Vegas, Nevada, October 2017

Above: Addressing the nation at the Republican National Convention, Rose Garden, White House, August 25, 2020

osite top: Welcoming Indian
ne Minister Narendra Modi,
te House, June 2017

osite bottom: Greeting
ıch President Emmanuel
cron and First Lady Brigitte
cron, West Wing, White
ıse, April 2018

Australia state visit, Prime
ister Scott Morrison and his
e, Jenny Morrison, White
se, September 2019

om: With Queen Rania
ordan, West Wing, White
se, 2017

Top left: Digital Collectible, melaniatrump.com, Palm Beach, 2021

Top right: Love & Gratitude Customizable Necklace & Digital Collectible, Mother's Day, 2024

Bottom left: 45 Liberty Gold Digital Collectible, USAmemorabilia.com, Presidents Day, 2022

Bottom right: Christmas Ornament & Digital Collectible, 2023 disasters, and global incidents—that require immediate and compassionate responses.

M

During the first half of 2017, I split my time between New York, Washington, and Mar-a-Lago, managing my duties as First Lady and supporting my husband's administration. From waking Barron up in the morning to attending rallies and meeting with foreign leaders, every moment was filled with purpose and excitement. Juggling two full-time roles in different locations was exhausting but rewarding, and I embraced the challenge wholeheartedly.

Even before my move to Washington, I began establishing my office as the First Lady. Being an outsider, I had to assert myself gently and work with trusted individuals. The timeline was tight, and there was a lack of clarity on the budget, but we worked diligently to determine our resources and staffing capabilities. However, we encountered obstacles in securing the necessary support and resources, as competition within the team was evident. I remained focused on building a team that was dedicated to the mission and values of the office. While previous First Ladies' offices had as many as twenty-three staff, I never had more than twelve people on my team—large enough to do everything I wanted to do, but small enough to stay responsive, nimble, and effective.

We got off to a busy start. In early February, I attended an American Red Cross event in Florida to show my continued support for their important work. Shortly after, Donald and I hosted Japanese prime minister Shinzo Abe and his wife, Akie, at Mar-a-Lago, aiming to strengthen the crucial alliance between our countries. I had the pleasure of connecting with Akie and found her company delightful.

Finally, on February 18, I delivered my first official speech as First Lady at a rally in Florida, introducing my husband, the president, to the audience, and reintroducing myself to the nation.

As Donald and I prepared to disembark Air Force One at the Orlando airport, the sight of the thousands gathered below, chanting and cheering our names, was a powerful reminder of the trust and support the American people had placed in us.

Their steadfast loyalty, even after the election, was a poignant testament to the faith they had in our leadership. It was a humbling experience to witness their enthusiasm and encouragement, which served as a reminder of the responsibility we carried.

M

In preparation for our move to Washington, D.C., I had been researching schools for Barron and making arrangements to ensure the White House felt like a comfortable and welcoming home for our family. While the logistics of relocating can be challenging, my priority was to create a sense of stability and familiarity for Barron during this transition. I was dedicated to ensuring that he had a smooth and positive experience.

Unfortunately, my plans to begin preparing the residence before the inauguration were disrupted by protocols and politics. It is customary for the incoming first family to start the moving process when the outgoing first family leaves for the holidays in December, and I understand the importance of following tradition in this manner. Sadly, our team did not receive the access we had requested to visit the White House residence in December. Despite reaching out to the Obamas' team and requesting a convenient time for our visit, we did not receive a response for weeks. When we finally received the information, it was filled with errors. This delayed the planning process, and I was only able to begin renovations after the inauguration, once we were already in the White House. Those three weeks would have been crucial for taking measurements, gathering plans, and starting preparations.

Each first family has the opportunity to decorate and personalize certain rooms on the residential floors of the White House according to their taste. They are able to choose furniture from a catalog provided by the White House warehouse, bring their own items from home, or purchase new furniture using approved funds. This allows the first family to create a comfortable and welcoming living space while respecting the historical significance of the White House.

Redecorating from a distance posed its challenges, but with the expertise of talented New York–based interior designer Tham Kannalikham, the project was a success. With her knowledge in history and preservation, I knew she would be the perfect partner for the job. Knowing I couldn't do everything at once, I planned to gradually expand my renovating and redecorating efforts throughout the White House.

We initially focused on redecorating a dozen rooms in the private residence, as the existing style was outdated or not to my taste. Barron's room was a priority. He was the first young boy to live in the White House since John Kennedy Jr., and the children's bedrooms had been decorated for girls for sixty years, so it was important to create a space that suited Barron's interests.

Before our move to the White House, I brought Barron to visit a few times to help him adjust to his new surroundings. We decorated his room together and brought familiar items from New York to make him feel more comfortable. In May, we hosted his New York classmates for a visit, which included lunch at the White House and a tour of the Oval Office. Barron was excited and proud to show his friends where he would be living. He enjoyed the White House and was looking forward to calling it home.

The transition on June 11, 2017 to the White House was a momentous occasion for our family. The iconic symbol served as a reminder of the responsibilities and opportunities that lay ahead. It was a day filled with excitement and anticipation for the journey that awaited us.

The exceptional staff made us feel right at home and, by the time we settled in, everything felt in place. My office in the residence and the Yellow Oval Room became favorite spots for work and relaxation, although our busy schedules meant we rarely had time for TV, other than the news, as we were always on the move or working.

Access to the residential areas of the White House is highly restricted, only granted to those invited by the first family. However, public spaces on the first floor and outdoor areas require strict organization, security measures, and adherence to protocol, ensuring utmost safety. Privacy is limited in these shared spaces.

I reassured Barron that our family would make the White House our home and face the challenges together, as a family. I admired his resilience during the transition, as moving to a new house in a new city can be tough for anyone, let alone a sixth grader. The limitations of being constantly under Secret Service protection and living in the public eye made everyday activities more complicated. We were prepared for the increased public attention on Barron's life, knowing that being the president's son brought a whole new level of scrutiny.

The summer move facilitated a smoother adjustment for us. With the school year over and Barron occupied with soccer camp, we had the opportunity to settle in before the start of the new school year in September. As the first family, our duty was to support my husband, who had been elected to lead the country. The timing felt right, and we were all looking forward to serving together.

M

Upon moving into the White House, it became evident that the historic building was in need of proper care and attention. Its grandeur and beauty were undeniable, yet a sense of neglect lingered in the air.

As the President's residence, a symbol of our equality, opportunity, protection and strength, and a home for our family, it was imperative to ensure that the White House was well-maintained. Recognizing the significance of this responsibility, I took it upon myself as First Lady to oversee the upkeep of the property. After all, the White House is not just our home—it is the people's house, a house of democracy and pride. And so, with a sense of reverence and dedication, I set out to restore this national treasure.

The White House is not just a museum, it is a living space with over 130 rooms that require some adjustment. The layout is relatively simple, with different areas designated for specific purposes. The residence spans the second and third floors, while the ground floor houses offices and reception rooms. During my initial days at the White House, I was always accompanied by a team of staff and security personnel to help me navigate the space. This allowed me to quickly familiarize myself with the layout and understand the work that needed to be done. My goal was to preserve the historical significance of the White House while also creating a modern and inviting home. I strove to strike a balance between maintaining the integrity of its history and ensuring it felt fresh and beautiful in the present day.

In every room you enter, in every detail, you feel that the White House is steeped in history. Everything tells a story, you can't help but sense how much the house has witnessed over the years. It has seen battles, fires, expansions, and reconstructions, not to mention more than two centuries of first families.

Over the years, I had undertaken numerous renovation projects in our apartment in Trump Tower and our home in Florida. I was well-versed in handling planning and design work independently, thanks to my background and education in design and architecture. I brought this expertise to the White House, but given the historic nature of the building I needed a team of highly skilled and knowledgeable architects and designers. That is where Tham Kannalikham came in once again. We shared a design sensibility that favored classic, understated elegance over anything gaudy or loud. Tham understood the White House's potential and the extent of the work required. Her calm energy and profound knowledge of American history, design, and decorative arts made her an invaluable partner. She respected the White House as much as I did and was always eager to learn more.

The extensive renovations we envisioned for the White House had not been done in many years. While some first families are content to simply live in the historic residence, my approach was different. Detailed planning and coordination were essential for any work in the White House. Budgetary approval, consent from historians and conservationists, and consultation with White House experts were all necessary steps before beginning any project. It required a significant amount of time and preparation to even get a project off the ground. We understood that some projects would be easier than others, so we started with those.

In the process of revitalizing the Green Room, we found that simply refreshing the draperies was all that was necessary to restore its charm. However, in the case of the Red Room, the vibrant Scalamandré silk on the walls had faded to a dull pink and the upholstery on the chairs had become ragged and worn. To remedy this, we took the initiative to send the furniture out for reupholstering and replaced the fabric on the walls. As a result, the Red Room has been restored to its original red glory once again.

The White House is maintained by several organizations such as the White House Historical Association, the Committee for the Preservation of the White House, and the National Park Service. These groups play a crucial role in the ongoing upkeep efforts of the White House. However, the decision on where to focus these efforts ultimately lies with the First Lady. My guidance and input were essential in determining the preservation and maintenance priorities of this historic landmark.

Throughout the months, I continued to enhance the Yellow Oval Room at the White House. I carefully selected beautiful antiques from the White House collection, such as an eighteenth-century French table and a gilded candelabra, to complement the new curtains and sofas. I personally designed a custom rug featuring American Beauty roses, blue ribbons, and a trellis motif to tie everything together. These small details made a significant impact, revitalizing the old rooms and infusing them with new life.

The restoration project of the President's Dining Room on the second floor of the White House involved a fascinating discovery that had historians excited. A leak had caused damage to the wallpaper, which had been covered up by a decorator in the past. Upon removing the fabric, we uncovered a wall of priceless Zuber wallpaper, which had also sustained water damage. I brought in conservators who were able to carefully remove and restore the wallpaper, with plans to eventually move it to a museum. It was truly remarkable to be a part of uncovering this piece of history and witnessing the layers of the past come to light.

We completed a comprehensive renovation of the Queen's Bedroom, which had not been updated in many years. This historic room has hosted important guests such as Queen Elizabeth II and

Winston Churchill, but was in need of modernization. The outdated bathroom, untouched since the 1950s, was given a much-needed update. We replaced the old bed with a more refined piece, laid a lighter, floral-patterned rug, and painted the walls a delicate shade of pink. The room now feels feminine, refreshed, and ready to welcome future dignitaries.

As anyone who knows me will attest, I am meticulously organized and thrive on having a clear plan. This allowed us to have several projects running concurrently, each at different stages of completion. One significant endeavor was the months-long restoration of the East Room floor. Worn and scuffed from years of use, the floor required painstaking work to re-create its intricate pattern. The talented craftspeople executed this task with remarkable skill and dedication. Watching their precision and artistry was truly inspiring.

Undertaking renovations in the White House is never straightforward. The logistics are complex, and the workers' patience was commendable. For instance, if renovations were underway in the private residence and Donald came home, the crew would have to stop work and leave the area. I could remain, but due to security protocols, the president could not be present during the work. The crew would pause for as long as needed, sometimes just until Donald finished a phone call, and then seamlessly resumed their tasks. Their unflappable nature in the face of such interruptions was remarkable, and I am profoundly grateful for their efforts. None of our achievements would have been possible without their dedication.

Among our many projects, we successfully upgraded the curators' area to meet museum-standard storage requirements. This enhancement ensures that proper care, restoration, and documentation are prioritized, safeguarding the integrity and value of our treasured items.

We restored the marble floors of the State Floor entrance and hallway, which are the first areas to greet visitors to the White House. We rejuvenated all the doors in the private residence, renewed handrails untouched since the Truman renovation, and revived the White House bowling alley, initially installed in the early seventies. This involved new flooring, updated wiring, and new balls and shoes. Once completed, I celebrated by hosting a party there for the children of our Secret Service agents—the joyful event that perfectly broke in the renewed space.

I was dedicated to seeing through the completion of the projects I initiated during my time in office. Renovations in historic settings can be lengthy, but I was determined that the projects bearing my name would be finished under my administration. The success of our team was greatly influenced by the guidance of the White House conservation and curatorial teams.

We all shared a common goal: to balance the preservation of the past with the needs of the present and to ensure the continuation of tradition well into the future. With this goal in mind, I designed a piece of a new rug for the Diplomatic Reception Room. The old rug had faded and was deteriorating from decades of foot traffic. I envisioned a replacement that would honor the past, the present, and the future of our country while also embodying my vision for the White House. Instead of the old rug's fifty state seals, the new design featured a presidential seal at the center, surrounded by a border of the fifty state flowers, celebrating the natural beauty and diversity of America. I believe that this rug, along with our other restoration projects, will be cherished for many years to come.

M

In 2018, I undertook the designing of a new White House Tennis Pavilion. The existing structure, a dilapidated shack ironically referred to as the Pony Shed, was wholly inadequate. It was important to create a space that not only served its functional purpose but also added to the aesthetic appeal of the White House. Preservation was not the goal; we aimed to construct a new and beautiful pavilion that would enhance the overall ambiance of the White House grounds.

Working once again with Tham and her team, we consulted architects, historians, designers, and tennis professionals to perfect the plans. We needed approval from various White House organizations: the Committee for the Preservation of the White House, the National Park Service, the General Services Administration, the U.S. Commission of Fine Arts, and the National Capital Planning Commission. In 2019, with the approvals in place, we began construction. The new tennis court and pavilion, funded entirely through a single private donation and built in partnership with the Trust for the National Mall and the National Parks Service, would be located on the south grounds. The pavilion would match the neo-classical style of the White House and feature floor-to-ceiling windows, locker rooms, and showers.

I was delighted when we had a groundbreaking ceremony for the new tennis pavilion project at the White House. It was an exciting opportunity to contribute to a legacy piece that will benefit future first families.

Despite the challenges brought on by the pandemic, our team continued to work tirelessly. We faced criticism for continuing the project during the pandemic, but many workers thanked me for not stopping, as it allowed their businesses to stay afloat. I chose to overlook the negativity and instead concentrate on the positive outcomes of our efforts. Building and preserving are always constructive endeavors, and my focus has always been on enhancing the beauty and history of the White House, rather than seeking recognition from the media.

M

Camp David, formally known as the Naval Support Facility Thurmont, was established in 1942 and has served as a presidential retreat since the Eisenhower administration. Located in the Catoctin Mountains of Maryland, it has played a pivotal role in various historical events.

The operational management of Camp David involves a close collaboration with military staff, primarily from the U.S. Navy, who oversee the facility's security and logistical needs. This relationship is characterized by a commitment to maintaining confidentiality and ensuring the safety of presidential activities. The military staff at Camp David are trained to support the unique demands of the retreat, providing essential services while fostering an environment conducive to high-level discussions.

The architectural design of Camp David reflects a blend of rustic charm and functional simplicity, drawing inspiration from early American architecture. The main lodge, known as Aspen Lodge, is where the president resides while there.

During my visit to Camp David, I observed that the lodge required updates. I reached out to the military team, and they expressed appreciation for my willingness to assist with the improvements. The protocol mandated that all plans receive military approval prior to commencement.

We successfully renovated all rooms and upgraded the digital wiring and heating systems.

We preserved its original character, which is essential for maintaining the integrity and authenticity of Camp David. It not only honors the historical significance but also enhances the overall aesthetic and functional value, ensuring a harmonious blend of tradition and modernity.

M

Our team's work on the Rose Garden was a point of pride for all involved. This iconic garden, located just outside the Oval Office, holds a rich history that dates back to its beginnings as a small rose house. Over the years, it has evolved into a grand garden thanks to the guidance of landscape architect Frederick Law Olmsted Jr. during the FDR administration, and a later redesign by Jackie Kennedy in the early 1960s.

Sixty years later, there were several issues that needed addressing. The Committee for the Preservation of the White House, which had commissioned a study on the garden, approached me for my approval. Our planning included a new limestone walkway to provide ADA accessibility during events, an upgraded irrigation system, digital wiring, and soil revitalization.

The Rose Garden is a testament to the legacy of First Ladies, and it was my privilege to select and oversee the installation of "Floor Frame," a sculpture by Isamu Noguchi, the first work by an Asian American artist in the White House collection. This modern piece, with its strength, simplicity, and balanced design, seamlessly complements the garden, embodying themes of resilience and renewal.

As First Lady, I eventually found a natural rhythm. My schedule was unrelenting, filled with trips, meetings, and commitments, but the ongoing work of restoring the White House provided comforting continuity. These projects, executed quietly and without fanfare, were my part of contributing something lasting and beautiful to the

American people, transcending politics and partisanship. They were a testament to my dedication to preserving the history and beauty of the White House for future generations.

Chapter 12

Welcome to the White House

From state dinners to official parties, I strove to orchestrate every detail to perfection.

Our first formal party as president and First Lady was the Governors Ball, an annual black-tie event held in late February for the nation's governors and their spouses, who were in town for their annual meeting. Technically, the president and First Lady are cohosts, but as with many White House events, the details and execution are largely the responsibility of the First Lady. This was my first major event, and I wanted it to be perfect.

Without much time between the inauguration and the ball, I quickly got to work on preparations, collaborating with talented designer and event planner David Monn. Embracing the idea of "Spring's Renewal," I encouraged unity in a statement before the event, urging guests to set aside political differences. As our guests arrived, including governors from both parties, we welcomed them in the Blue Room. The State Dining Room was beautifully decorated for the occasion, and the evening was a great success. The event brought together Democrats and Republicans, striving for a positive tone for future collaborations.

A First Lady's annual event calendar is always full, and as I gained experience planning and hosting White House events, I became more comfortable with the range of special occasions that called for my creative involvement.

In February, on Valentine's Day, I had the pleasure of visiting the children at the hospital run by the NIH. We shared in the joy of making crafts together and indulging in some sweet treats. Comforting children was one of the most rewarding aspects of my role as First Lady.

In March, I hosted a luncheon for International Women's Day, where we discussed the challenges faced by women worldwide, a cause that is close to my heart. I also had the privilege of speaking at the International Women of Courage Award Ceremony at the State Department. I was inspired by the stories of these incredible individuals, from a woman who stood up against early and forced marriages in Bangladesh, to an activist who helps provide shelter and support for women escaping violence and oppression in Iraq.

While the Easter Egg Roll has the playful atmosphere of a picnic, state dinners are decidedly formal affairs. I chose to take a hands-on approach to planning the first state dinner. While many opt to delegate this task to outside teams or staff members, I felt confident in my abilities and wanted to ensure that each event was executed to my standards. The purpose of a state dinner is to host foreign leaders, following a strict protocol of events and ceremonies. I was determined to make the state dinner for French President Emmanuel Macron and his wife, Brigitte, a memorable and elegant affair.

Brigitte and I shared a delightful camaraderie, marked by warmth and fun. Our interactions were enjoyable and we were always glad to see each other. Together, we embraced the unknown, turning every moment into an exciting adventure.

France is a vital ally to the United States, and hosting a dinner for the Macrons highlighted the importance of our relationship. Donald's and Emmanuel's open communication and mutual respect were the cornerstones of their partnership. They showed that a great personal relationship is crucial in achieving success for our countries.

Donald and I welcomed the French president and First Lady with a reception on the South Lawn of the White House ahead of our official state dinner that evening. For the welcome, in a nod to the meeting of French and American leaders, I wore a suit by Michael Kors and a hat designed for me by the French American designer Hervé Pierre. For dinner that evening, I paid further homage to our guest's country by wearing an exquisite silver Chanel gown.

From the china and the flowers to the table settings and entertainment, I wanted every detail of the evening's setting to reflect connection between the United States and France. I felt pressured to get everything exactly right, especially the seating arrangements, but I embraced the challenge with enthusiasm. The inclusion of French artists, delicious cuisine and music, businessmen, and other distinguished guests epitomized the strong and enduring partnership between our nations.

M

Every year, I would begin planning for Christmas, a very special holiday to me, in early July. It was a lot to oversee and I ensured that every detail was meticulously coordinated.

Christmas season at the White House is a highly anticipated event. It begins on the North entrance, when I accept the Christmas tree the day before Thanksgiving. During the holiday weekend, dedicated volunteers from across the nation assist in decorating the residence. After returning from Thanksgiving at Mar-a-Lago, I was looking forward to seeing my creations coming to life.

The following day, we opened the White House to the public and hosted several gatherings. Donald and I addressed the visitors and took photos with military, Secret Service, residence staff families, and officials from the cabinet and government.

Chapter 13

Be Best

"We have to find a better way to talk to each other, to disagree with each other, to respect each other. We must find better ways to honor and support the basic goodness of our children, especially in social media. It will be one of the main focuses of my work if I'm privileged enough to become your First Lady."

I had spoken those words in Berwyn, Pennsylvania, on November 3, 2016, five days before Donald won the election.

Technology, I told the audience, while a powerful tool, brings significant dangers. The landscape had changed so dramatically since my own childhood, and children were struggling to navigate it. There was so little supervision, so few guardrails, and no real regulation. Our children were not equipped to handle the kind of bullying enabled by social media, which is often anonymous, targeted, and extraordinarily cruel. Adults have failed to address this crisis, and children were suffering. As a mother, I found this unacceptable. I had long felt that we were sleepwalking into a very dangerous situation.

I had first addressed the dangers of cyberbullying even earlier, in an interview with Anderson Cooper in October 2016. "My passion,"

I told him, "is helping children and helping women. And seeing [it] now, in the twenty-first century—with social media—it's very damaging for children."

We seem to be living in an age where much of our lives is presented for public consumption on social media. Some moments in life are meant to be private and do not need to be shared with the world. Personally, I have always valued my privacy and have been cautious about what I share online. During my time in the White House, I made sure to only post official activities and destinations. Having experienced the scrutiny of the public eye, I understand the challenges that come with living in a world where everything is on display. These challenges are all magnified when it comes to children. It's painfully evident to all parents that the internet, social media, and prevalent online harassment are posing a substantial risk to the mental and emotional health of our children.

I experienced firsthand the poison of social media when my son became the target of a concerted cyberbullying campaign. Two weeks after the election, Rosie O'Donnell took to Twitter to pose a "question" to her millions of followers: "Barron Trump Autistic? If so, what an amazing opportunity to bring attention to the AUTISM epidemic. #StopTheBullying."

I was appalled by such cruelty. It was clear to me that she was not interested in raising awareness about autism. I felt that she was attacking my son because she didn't like my husband. It all began when Donald extended a helping hand to Miss USA, offering her the support she desperately needed to overcome her addiction. This powerful act of kindness not only changed her life but also sent a powerful message: that with compassion and understanding, we can help others rise from their struggles.

Rosie's tweet alone was irresponsible and hurtful, but the worst part was the video O'Donnell linked to a seven-minute video of Barron at various events over the years. Someone had painstakingly compiled the footage and added captions like "His hands are moving erratically and aren't touching each other. Then he was spotted making strange movements in his seat, typical of children with autism." In reality, Barron was simply behaving like any other child his age.

The tweet and video targeting Barron were not only cruel and invasive but also completely unfounded. There is nothing shameful about autism (though O'Donnell's tweet implied that there was), but Barron is not autistic. To float such a "question" to a million people, knowing exactly how it would be received, was beyond careless; it was heartless. Bullying a ten-year-old is egregious, but doing so under the flimsy pretense of "bringing awareness" to a condition many people genuinely suffer from was truly repulsive.

The sheer malice of O'Donnell's act made me furious. There was a child at the other end of that tweet. I felt awful for Barron, who had done nothing to deserve such treatment, especially from adults. I knew the tweet and video would go viral and I knew how much it would hurt him. As a parent, it was devastating to see my child targeted in such a way. It felt like my heart was breaking into pieces.

O'Donnell issued an apology a few days after her bullying message, but the impact of her tweet was undeniable. It is unfathomable to me that she, as a mother herself, could not foresee the consequences of her words on a young boy. Barron's experience of being bullied both online and in real life following the incident is a clear indication of the irreparable damage caused. No apology can undo the harm inflicted upon him.

I underscored the urgency and importance of doing more to safeguard our children from the pervasive dangers of the digital world. I wasn't alone in grappling with the effects of online bullying on children. Many parents were facing similar challenges, and it was clear that much more needed to be done to educate people, pressure social media and tech companies, and teach children how to protect themselves.

As First Lady, in September 2017, I hosted a luncheon at the U.S. Mission to the United Nations and delivered a speech on the perils of cyberbullying. "No child should ever feel hungry, stalked, frightened, terrorized, bullied, isolated or afraid, with nowhere to turn," I empathized. "We must teach each child the values of empathy and communication that are at the core of kindness, mindfulness, integrity, and leadership."

I was keenly aware of how perilous the online world could be: adults preying on children, cyberbullying among peers, abuse, gossip, and relentless peer pressure. Parents alone cannot monitor every aspect of their child's online activity. As First Lady, I believed I could contribute to a solution by shining a light on these complex issues and exerting my influence on tech companies to address them.

In March 2018, I convened a roundtable discussion with executives from major tech companies including Facebook, Google, Amazon, Snapchat, and Twitter. Meeting them in the State Dining Room in the White House, I sought insights and solutions. I wanted to work alongside them, learn what their companies were doing, understand their approach to the issue, and foster a constructive dialogue. Rather than presenting a list of demands, I approached the discussion as both a concerned mother and as First Lady, eager to explore effective solutions. My main concern centered on the need for greater oversight of children's online activities and communication. Based on my observations, much of the most severe online bullying was perpetrated anonymously. This anonymity further facilitated expressions of racism, sexism, and cruelty that would be unacceptable in face-to-face interactions. I urged the tech companies to consider measures that could mitigate such harmful behavior and content.

I was taken aback by the resistance I encountered from the tech executives. They seemed to suggest that their ability to address harmful content was limited, due to concerns about free speech. I emphasized that I was not advocating for censorship, but rather for the protection of children from potentially harmful speech. Although the response from the tech companies was disappointing. I remained undeterred. I knew that even if these companies were not fully supportive, parents across the country would be. And I was correct. As I began to explore the issue more publicly, I heard from many parents who shared their fears, stories, and experiences with me. One encounter that particularly moved me was meeting a father in the White House whose son had taken his own life after being bullied online. His story was heartbreaking and underscored the urgency of the situation. Hearing from so many parents deepened my understanding and strengthened my resolve to use my platform to advocate for change.

I decided to launch an overarching initiative aimed at implementing impactful changes to ensure the well-being of our children. Determined to take my case directly to the people, this program would involve speaking directly with Americans—parents and children alike—about the dangers and risks facing children. I would partner with community groups and invite people to the White House to share their experiences and resources. My goal was to learn from them and to offer support and solutions. To enhance the visibility and impact of this new initiative, I worked on developing a distinctive logo and brand that would convey our shared goal of addressing online bullying and, more generally, the well-being of children. I called it, quite simply, Be Best.

On May 7, 2018, I delivered a speech in the Rose Garden to officially launch Be Best. This program was designed to address online safety and other critical issues affecting women and children. "As a mother and as First Lady," I said, "it concerns me that in today's fast-paced and ever-connected world, children can be less prepared to express or manage their emotions and oftentimes turn to forms of destructive or addictive behavior such as bullying, drug addiction, or even suicide. So today I'm very excited to announce Be Best, an awareness campaign dedicated to the most valuable and fragile among us, our children."

I outlined the three pillars of the initiative as I envisioned them: the well-being of children, online safety, and tackling opioid abuse, another crisis devastating mothers and children across the country.

"Together," I continued, "I believe we should strive to provide kids with the tools they need to cultivate their social and emotional health as we all know social media can both positively and negatively affect our children. But too often it is used in negative ways. It is our responsibility as adults to teach our children to use their voices with respect and compassion, to choose their words wisely." Be Best was my initiative, and I was proud to introduce it to the world. Knowing the importance of having Donald's support, I invited him to come to the podium for a few words. "America is truly blessed," he said, "to have a First Lady so devoted to our country and to our children. Everywhere she has gone, Americans have been touched by her sincerity, moved by her grace, and lifted by her voice."

"Today we pledge to Be Best," Donald concluded, before officially making May 7 Be Best Day.

I started receiving feedback from mothers immediately, and their responses were overwhelmingly positive. They expressed relief and gratitude: "Finally!" they said. "Thank you for bringing this issue up front." Parents understood the importance of protecting their children, and they appreciated someone speaking out. The desire to safeguard our children clearly transcends political divides.

I had anticipated some criticism in light of Donald's social media behavior, but despite the scrutiny my stance might receive, addressing this issue was a personal priority for me. Throughout the campaign and his presidency, I maintained that my advocacy wouldn't be swayed by how my husband managed his Twitter account. Helping parents and children address the challenges of the digital age was my focus. I firmly believed that we would be able to teach children to navigate this digital landscape responsibly.

In addition to raising awareness, my goals were to mobilize resources and help children.

I was heartened to see the quick support and interest in the Be Best initiative from organizations like the Family Online Safety Institute and the National PTA Legislative Conference. Collaborating with these established groups and experts in the field of child well-being was crucial for the sustainability of our efforts. It was also encouraging to hear from First Ladies globally, such as Brigitte Macron and Queen Mathilde of Belgium, who expressed their admiration for my Be Best initiative and shared plans to start similar endeavors of their own.

I exchanged ideas with Queen Mathilde, with whom I'd attended a forum on preventing the exploitation of children online during my visit to her country. I felt confident that this collaborative approach would strengthen our collective impact in helping children globally.

However, following the launch of Be Best, the media attempted to diminish this remarkable initiative by focusing on its title. Critics questioned the grammar, suggesting alternatives like "Be Your Best" or "Be The Best." I chose #BeBest intentionally. It struck a chord with me and projected strength, positivity, and confidence. Its catchy, memorable, and unique nature set it apart.

M

I knew early on that the opioid epidemic was an area where Be Best could make a difference. For years, I had been deeply moved by the stories of individuals struggling with addiction. The devastating impact of this crisis on families, especially young mothers and children, was clear. In September 2017, I hosted a roundtable at the White House focused on opioid addiction, where I listened to the heartbreaking stories of recovering addicts, parents of overdose victims, and addiction and recovery professionals. One couple shared the story of their desperate efforts to save their son from addiction, only to lose him to an overdose.

After attending the roundtable on the opioid crisis, I visited Lily's Place, an infant recovery center in Huntington, West Virginia, to gain a deeper understanding of neonatal abstinence syndrome, a condition in which newborns experience opioid withdrawal because their mothers were addicted to opioids during pregnancy. Witnessing the suffering of these newborns was truly heartbreaking. The stories I heard highlighted the devastating impact of the crisis on families.

By 2019, Be Best was gaining significant traction, particularly in its efforts to combat cyberbullying. My discussions with Microsoft's top executives, president Brad Smith and CEO Satya Nadella, about implementing parental controls for Xbox, showed great promise.

At the same time, we were making progress in expanding Be Best's reach and impact to help even more individuals, specifically in regard to opioid addiction.

With Be Best, our overall objective was to bring attention to important issues impacting children and spark conversations about how to address them. While we knew these challenges wouldn't be solved quickly, it has been promising to see more people recognizing the importance of this cause. Florida's recent law restricting social media accounts for children under fourteen is one positive step forward in protecting our youth; the US surgeon general's call for warning labels on social media is another.

When I came to the White House, I reflected on the responsibility I have always felt as a mother to encourage, give strength, and teach values of kindness. It is our duty as adults and parents to ensure that children have the best opportunities to lead fulfilling and healthy lives. I launched Be Best to ensure that we as Americans are doing everything we can to take care of the next generation. There is always more to be done, but I am immensely proud of the fact that in a few short years, my initiative raised awareness of how to keep children safe online, made incredible progress on understanding our nation's drug epidemic and how it impacts the lives of newborns and families, and gave a voice to our most vulnerable children. Internationally, Be Best evolved into a platform that encourages world leaders to discuss issues impacting the lives of children and allows them to share solutions.

Chapter 14

Going Global

Any official presidential trip abroad requires an unimaginable amount of planning and coordination. Security, protocol, personalities! The level of preparation leading up to our journey to Saudi Arabia, Israel, Rome, Belgium, and Sicily in May 2017 was truly extraordinary.

The collaboration between the State Department, the West Wing, and the East Wing was complex and required meticulous attention to detail. As First Lady, I understood the importance of highly choreographed travel and was prepared for the extensive schedule that awaited us. I made it known to my chief of staff, Lindsay Reynolds, that I was eager to visit hospitals and schools during our trip, and I was pleased to see these visits included in my packed itinerary. The planning and execution of such a trip is truly a team effort, involving dozens of staff members and months of work.

The staff at the State Department expertly assembles a binder that tells you not only everything you'll be doing—hour to hour, minute to minute—but everything you might need to know about the countries to which you'll be traveling, such as cultural considerations, detailed descriptions of the places you'll visit, and biographical information about who you'll be meeting. I did my best to study all the details. I suppose preparation at that depth of detail might have made some people nervous, but I found all the information fascinating. It was work—being First Lady was always work—but I also thought of it as a welcome opportunity to expand my knowledge. A foreign trip with the president and First Lady is a delicate operation, sure to be scrutinized by the global media. It is important to avoid embarrassing diplomatic mistakes that might distract from the important issues at hand. I was looking forward to making the most of this wealth of information as we built these new and important relationships.

Departing from Washington in the evening, we flew overnight to minimize time in transit. We were also hoping to get some rest on the flight, since it would be important to be fully alert and focused upon landing. This journey marked a significant shift in our perception of travel. Before Donald became president, we had enjoyed quick getaways as a family of three, but now any travel involved an extensive operation with two full planes of individuals including staffers, reporters, and security guards. The atmosphere surrounding our trip to Saudi Arabia was filled with anticipation. There was some concern that the welcome could be unfriendly because of the travel restrictions Donald had placed on several countries in the Muslim world, places that he felt weren't taking terrorism seriously enough. This was the first Muslim country we'd visit, and there was much scrutiny as the media watched our every move.

King Salman bin Abdulaziz Al Saud greeted us at the International Airport in Riyadh with warmth and respect, breaking tradition as he greeted me. I had been warned that it wasn't Muslim tradition to shake hands with women and that the king might not extend me the courtesy. But when we met, he not only shook my hand but kissed it! This was a promising start! As is customary for the First Lady, I had carefully selected meaningful gifts for our hosts, a tradition I took great care to uphold. The gifts we received in return, which I often didn't see, went directly to the State Department, but giving and receiving was a proper display of diplomatic protocol.

We were attended by robed men in their traditional attire, the *thawb*, as we lounged in the comfortable seats while we sipped on the fragrant tea we had been offered as a traditional gesture of hospitality.

Donald was chauffeured with His Majesty while I had my own vehicle. When I entered the car, the princess was seated to my left, offering a warm smile in greeting. We chatted about her family and her beautiful country, with its stunning landscapes and rich history.

The route from the airport to central Riyadh was adorned with Saudi and US flags, as well as balloons representing other Muslim countries participating in the Arab-Islamic-American summit the following day.

I took videos and photos from the car, capturing the beauty of the scene. Upon my arrival at Al Yamamah Palace, I rejoined Donald and the king, while the princess returned to her own home. We were warmly welcomed with another reception during which King Salman presented Donald with the Collar of the Order of Abdulaziz Al Saud, the highest honor.

The official welcome ceremony took place later at the royal offices, where we were greeted by a procession of horsemen bearing Saudi and American flags who escorted the presidential Beast, which had been transported to Saudi Arabia for our security, as is protocol.

We toured Murabba Historical Palace, where traditional sword dancers invited Donald to join them in their performance. The day concluded with a celebratory banquet held in the courtyard, featuring traditional music.

The following day, while my husband attended to his busy schedule of meetings, I seized the opportunity to visit the prestigious American International School. In the absence of a traditional First Lady in Saudi Arabia, I ventured solo, accompanied only by my team. The encounters with the students and educators left enduring memories.

As I explored Riyadh, I couldn't help but notice the absence of women in many spaces. It is one of the most striking things in this part of the world. Everywhere I went, men predominated, highlighting the cultural differences in this mostly Muslim society. While I respected the cultural norms, I couldn't help but empathize with the women of Saudi Arabia, whose freedoms are limited.

One rare exception to this was the General Electric All-Women Business Process & IT Services Center. Clad in elegant black attire, veiled in the traditional fashion, the women there diligently worked at their computers, a heartwarming sight in a nation where too many women are denied entry into the workforce. Though their faces were concealed by niqabs, their eyes gleamed with a fierce intellect and exquisite beauty, leaving a profound impression on me.

While I have long upheld the value of traditional gender roles—acknowledging the innate differences between men and women—I was thinking about how best to leverage my platform to champion women's empowerment. My own independence has always been very valuable to me. Having established successful careers both before and during my marriage, knowing that I can stand on my own if necessary, gives me great confidence in everything I do. I am convinced that increased female leadership in companies, corporations, and countries fosters a better, safer, and kinder world.

Leaving Saudi Arabia, we arrived in Israel on the morning of May 22, and we were graciously welcomed by Sara and Benjamin Netanyahu at Ben Gurion Airport. It was a pleasure to reconnect with Bibi and

Sara, whom Donald has known for a long time, and whom we had the pleasure of hosting in Washington earlier that year. I had thoroughly enjoyed my time with Sara during our visit to the National Museum of African American History and Culture, and I was excited to visit her country and to explore this new and unique destination. Israel was a stark contrast from Saudi Arabia, and I looked forward to the experiences that awaited us during our visit.

"The media hate us," Sara said to me as we stepped away from the plane, "but the people love us."

"We have that in common," I replied.

The media's obsession with sensationalizing trivial gestures was evident as they distorted a simple moment between myself and my husband. As we walked down the red carpet, I gently waved away his attempt to hold my hand. The media labeled it as a "swat" and used it as supposed evidence of marital discord. This false narrative had been perpetuated since the beginning of the campaign, and it was disheartening to see how eager people were to believe in it. It was a stark reminder of the extent to which the media could misrepresent even the most insignificant actions.

The occurrence, dubbed a "swat" by the gossipmongers, was a mere misunderstanding. Protocol demanded that the president and prime minister walk side by side, with their spouses trailing behind. Yet, unforeseen circumstances led to a slight deviation from the norm. Bibi ended up holding his wife's hand, and my husband walked beside them—three abreast. The red carpet simply could not accommodate all four of us abreast. I allowed my husband to continue walking with the prime minister and his wife, opting to take a step back. When he reached out to offer his hand, I declined, indicating that I was perfectly content walking on my own. It was a minor innocent gesture, nothing more.

There were clearly far more interesting topics to discuss.

Our schedule, as always, was filled to the brim. We were set to visit the Western Wall and the Church of the Holy Sepulchre, two of the holiest sites in the world.

While Donald would be engaged in these diplomatic endeavors, I was scheduled to visit the Hadassah Medical Center to spend time with children, distributing books and games. I was especially looking forward to this visit and was delighted that Sara would be joining me. Our first stop was an outdoor playground where we met with pediatric patients and nurses. Along the way, we passed a bench that had been dedicated in honor of our visit.

M

After Israel, we were off to Rome—much more familiar ground for me. Italy has always held a special place in my heart. It was where my family would vacation, where I participated in one of my earliest modeling competitions, and where I first lived independently, in Milan, at the beginning of my career. I have wonderful memories of Italy and had explored much of the country, including the Vatican, which I visited with my parents as a child. Visiting now as First Lady, I was looking forward to meeting the pope for the first time, which was a special occasion for me as a Catholic. In preparation for this meeting, I carefully thought about the significance of the event. My family has a deep connection to our faith, with my grandmother and mother upholding important Catholic traditions. As a symbol of my faith and marriage, I brought a rosary with me, hoping for a blessing from the pope. In a nod to Italy's rich history and influence in the fashion world, I decided to wear a black lace Dolce & Gabbana coat and dress with a matching veil.

During our meeting in the Vatican's Sala del Tronetto, also known as the Little Throne Room, I humbly requested Pope Francis's blessing on my rosary, and he graciously obliged, offering a prayer over the sacred beads. In a gentle voice and with a warm smile, he then asked me, referring to my husband:

"What do you give him to eat? *Potica?*"

"Yes, pizza," I replied, not fully hearing him. Then I realized he was inquiring about *potica*, the traditional Slovenian pastry.

"Oh yes, *potica*." I smiled, touched by his effort to connect with me personally. It was a humbling experience to engage with such a revered figure on a personal level, emphasizing the importance of building relationships through genuine interactions.

While Donald had a private meeting with the pope, I went to visit the Bambino Gesù Children's Hospital. I was greeted warmly by a group of children from different backgrounds, who were able to engage in social activities and play games without any challenges. It was humbling and inspiring to see their strength in the face of illness.

I vividly recall a tender encounter with a young boy, merely eight years old, surrounded by lifesaving machines. His delicate face, barely visible beneath a sheer veil, awaited the miracle of a heart transplant. The doctors gravely explained the urgency of his situation, his life hanging in the balance. Standing by his bedside, I fought back tears, offering my support in any way I could. I felt powerless in the face of such fragility and I longed to ease his suffering, but all we could do was wait. The medical team promised to sustain him until a suitable heart could be found. As I gently reached out to touch him, I whispered a fervent prayer for his recovery. It was a heart-wrenching moment, a moment having nothing to do with the fervent politics of the US or the world, for that matter.

The experience with the young boy at the Vatican-run hospital returned my thoughts to my own child. This trip marked the longest

I had ever been away from Barron. Though I knew he was in loving hands with my parents, I still felt the ache of our separation. Every evening, I made it a point to call him. His innocent voice filled me with longing as he eagerly awaited my return.

Then, a miracle unfolded. . . . on the plane to Belgium, news arrived that a heart had been found for a young boy from Greece, whom I had personally met and held hands with. The sheer joy that filled my heart at this remarkable development was indescribable.

In Brussels, we met with Queen Mathilde, who shared my concerns about online bullying. After attending an enlightening presentation on cyber safety by the Queen, I extended my gratitude to her. Her insights were not only valuable, but also immensely important.

We headed to our final stop: Taormina, Sicily, for a G7 meeting with leaders from the United Kingdom, Canada, France, Japan, Italy, and Germany.

After a military helicopter ride to Catania, Sicily, at the foot of Mount Etna, I was welcomed by the city's mayor along with the other First Ladies for a lunch at the Palazzo dei Chierici. It was great to have the opportunity to engage with other women who shared similar roles and responsibilities. Through our discussions, I observed that they had fewer security measures in place compared to what I faced, which granted them more flexibility in their movements. Their roles appeared to be less formal and demanding, and they were surprised by the level of responsibility and expectations placed on American First Ladies.

M

Toward the end of our first year in the White House, Donald and I embarked on our first official trip to Asia, stopping first in Hawaii before flying on to South Korea, Japan, and China. Upon arriving in China, we participated in a beautiful welcome ceremony at the airport, followed by a welcome tea and a couples dinner at the Forbidden City with President Xi and Madame Peng. We were fortunate, too, to have a private tour of the Forbidden City alongside President Xi and Madame Peng, during which we were able to go behind the scenes and see all the work that went into preserving such an important historical treasure. The organization and hard work on display were extremely impressive.

On the second day, Madame Peng and I toured the Banchang Primary School, where we participated in various classes, including Peking opera, astronomy, fashion and design, calligraphy, cooking, and Chinese architecture. Again, I was impressed by what I saw, especially the teaching of traditional crafts and skills. I also noticed that none of the children were on their phones. They were focused on their studies instead, disciplined, and very respectful. I was glad to have had the opportunity to visit a Chinese school.

Of course, I also understood that life in China differs from that in the United States—it is stricter and more closely monitored by the state. There is less freedom. But the people I met there were hard-working and courteous, and they clearly took great pride in their work and studies. It was a visit I will never forget. President Xi and Madame Peng were gracious hosts—she the warm, elegant former Opera singer, and he the tough, smart leader of a billion and a half people. I was honored to participate in many cultural experiences and personal conversations with them.

M

I have always been driven to help those in need, especially the most vulnerable, and I felt a strong sense of duty to use my platform as First Lady for good. This commitment, made at the beginning of my husband's presidency, only grew more important over time. With those thoughts in mind I completed the necessary preparations for my first solo foreign trip as our nation's First Lady.

I made the decision to elevate my Be Best initiative to a global platform. My mission was clear: to uplift and empower women and children, to foster understanding of goodwill and well-being. I planned to visit Ghana, Malawi, Kenya, and Egypt over a five-day period, with the intention of making a positive impact on the lives of women and children in these countries. I was eager to contribute, learn, and explore in any way possible.

My trip in October 2018 began with a visit that I felt profoundly marked our complicated history with the African continent. It was a poignant reminder of our collective human responsibility to mend the scars of our past.

The "Door of No Return" in Ghana is an ominous landmark, the final threshold for enslaved individuals before their forced journey across the ocean. I had studied history, read the accounts, and knew the grim facts, but I wanted to witness it for myself.

Upon arriving at Cape Coast Castle—one of the many European-built trading posts used during the Atlantic slave trade—I laid a wreath and reflected on lives irrevocably altered by this brutal chapter in human history. It's impossible not to be deeply moved by such a place.

My visit to the Greater Accra Regional Hospital was an especially rewarding experience. I had the opportunity to witness the care and treatment of newborns at the "Old Child Welfare Clinic," where babies were weighed and received vitamins and other essential services. I had the pleasure of cradling precious little ones in my arms and engaging in conversations with their mothers.

These moments stand out in my mind during my time as First Lady. It was a gift to be able to meet so many people, and maybe give a ray of hope to those whose lives are so different from the lives of most Americans.

It was an honor to tour the Private Neonatal Intensive Care Unit (NICU) in the hospital's new section alongside First Lady Rebecca Akufo-Addo and the hospital's medical director. At the end of our visit, the USAID Administrator and I presented a phototherapy machine, diapers, and weighing bags to the NICU. I was impressed at the level of dedication and commitment from the hospital staff in providing quality care to its most vulnerable patients.

From Ghana, we flew to Malawi, where we visited the Chipala Primary School in Lilongwe. I was taken aback by the sheer number of students and lack of teachers and adequate classrooms. Eighty educators taught nearly 8,500 students in only twenty classrooms, yet the students, seated in the hot sunshine, clad in their regal blue and brown uniforms, were enthusiastic and eager to learn. Their radiant smiles and thirst for knowledge were truly a sight to behold.

I sat in a reading session with a group of students in the hot sun. The children sat on the ground cross-legged, holding their books, as they echoed the teacher's words. Their positive spirit brought a smile to my face, but the poor condition of their school weighed heavily on my heart. The young child seated beside me, eagerly absorbing every word, clearly had a strong desire to learn. His eyes met mine, radiating warmth and passion for acquiring knowledge.

Before departing, I distributed soccer balls, school supplies, and Be Best tote bags stuffed with books. And I was elated to be present when the US ambassador announced a donation of 1.4 million books. "Be Best tote bags" may sound like nothing to us, but that was not the case in many of these impoverished places. Though a modest gesture, it was a testament to our promise to make a difference. The children happily demonstrated their soccer skills to me and my team. It was a joy to witness their laughter and competitive spirit when it came to the game.

As my trip in Africa continued, my appreciation for this beautiful continent grew stronger.

My visit to Kenya was also remarkable. It was a real thrill to feed the baby elephants at the Sheldrick Wildlife Trust orphanage, even though one nudged me, catching the attention of a Secret Service agent.

I was deeply touched by the kindness and resilience of the people I met, particularly when I met the children at the Nest Children's Home. Engaging with the children at the orphanage proved to be a truly fulfilling and emotional experience for both me and my team. I had an opportunity to play with infants and read to a group of children. I was asked to take my place in the center as the children gathered around me, their innocent faces filled with joy. Together, we formed a circle of pure intentions, ready to offer a prayer of unity and blessings. It was a moment of divine connection when their sweet voices intertwined with mine. And as we stood there, surrounded by their strong faith, I felt honored to be a part of such a sacred moment.

My final stop was Cairo, where I was warmly welcomed by President Abdel Fattah el-Sisi and his wife, Entissar Amer. We proceeded to the Presidential Palace through secure and empty streets, where President el-Sisi articulated a compelling vision for the future of Egypt. The historical insights and challenges shared by the minister of tourism were incredibly enlightening. Visiting the Pyramids at Giza and the Sphinx, two of the Seven Wonders of the World, was truly captivating. My visit was brief, and I wished I could have spent more time exploring this historically and culturally important country. Unfortunately, these international trips don't allow for much leisure time.

M

"I have said this before, but it's worth repeating. We know that we are free because you are brave, and I speak on behalf of my husband when I tell you we are forever grateful for your service. I also want to take a moment to recognize the families served."

I was addressing an audience of servicemen and women at Joint Base Langley-Eustis in Virginia. It was December 2018. Supporting our military is a fundamental belief of mine. I come from an area of the world that has experienced violence. Freedom must never be taken for granted. With Christmas approaching, I showed my support by visiting the base to engage with military personnel directly and to convey the depth of appreciation and support my husband and I had for them. "We know that you often endure time apart, which also comes with a degree of uncertainty," I said, "and some of you are here today while your loved ones are far away. Frequent moves and deployments can be hard, and that kind of lifestyle requires its own kind of incredible courage. Please know that your sacrifices do not go unnoticed or unappreciated and that the president and I thank you for all that you do."

After speaking to the brave soldiers on base, I boarded a V-22 Osprey aircraft for a flight over the Atlantic to the USS *George H.W. Bush*—a colossal $6.2 billion U.S. Navy aircraft carrier spanning 1,000 feet. Initially, all I could see was the ocean stretched out endlessly in all directions. As we neared the ship, it gradually grew until its true magnitude became apparent. What had seemed small on the horizon was now a feat of naval engineering looming before us. Only when we were directly above it did I fully comprehend the grand scale of the naval aircraft carrier. It resembled a bustling city afloat in the middle of the ocean, throbbing with activity—an awe-inspiring sight.

We landed on the deck and received a warm welcome. I embarked on a comprehensive ship tour and was privileged to meet the crew. Standing on the observation booth in the brisk cold wind, I observed as planes executed their daring takeoffs, maneuvers, and landings—a scene reminiscent of something from *Top Gun*, yet resoundingly real, powerful, and loud. The deafening roar of engines only added to the thrilling atmosphere. I commended the courageous pilots for their exceptional skills.

Yet the most profound impact on me came from interacting with the young sailors and crewmembers. I enjoyed engaging them in conversations, listening to their stories, and simply connecting with them to demonstrate our support. As I mentioned above, these men and women endure months away from their families, living aboard ship in a uniquely challenging lifestyle. It was an honor to spend time with them, just as it was an honor to visit wounded veterans at Walter Reed National Military Medical Center and to work with the American Red Cross to ensure care packages reached our soldiers abroad.

My role as First Lady had already brought me into contact with remarkable Americans—people from diverse backgrounds who are engaged in a variety of professions worldwide. Each encounter left a lasting impression. The military personnel, in particular, filled me with immense pride for our nation. I recognized the privilege of meeting such extraordinary individuals. In some ways they stayed with me—each and every incredible person I met as First Lady. To this day, I find myself thinking about them, wondering about the paths their lives have taken, and hoping they have found health, fulfillment, and peace.

Supporting our troops from Washington was important, but I soon found myself presented with a new opportunity to connect with them in a different context: we were heading to Iraq. The mission was conducted discreetly, with the flight under the cover of darkness. The purpose was to visit our soldiers and generals on the front lines to wish them a Merry Christmas. The goal was to maintain secrecy and return to Washington, D.C., before any information leaked.

It was Donald's idea, initially, but knowing how deeply I valued our troops, he asked me to join. In the past, it was customary for the president to go alone to visit troops in a war zone, without the company of the First Lady, but Donald wanted me with him, and I was honored to go.

Naturally, I was a little apprehensive. While the risks were minimized with the best protection available, my thoughts inevitably turned to my loved ones and the what-ifs. Nevertheless, as First Lady, I was determined to visit our troops in the field. They were the ones putting themselves in harm's way for our safety back home. Nearly fifteen years after the post-9/11 deployment to Iraq ordered by George W. Bush, the United States still maintained a presence of over five thousand service members in the region.

In light of recent developments, Donald had made the decision to withdraw two thousand American troops from Syria. As a show of support and gratitude, visiting those stationed abroad during the holiday season was a priority. While this would require a shift from our typical Christmas plans, it was a small gesture to show our appreciation for their service.

The trip had been carefully planned with absolute secrecy for weeks, and I'd only become aware of it in early December. Except for my parents and Barron, very few other people were informed. To ensure security, much of the preparation was executed at the last minute. We left the White House in the evening through the underground garage, bypassing our usual vehicle to avoid any indication that the president was on the move. Air Force One, instead of being on the tarmac at

Andrews, was hidden in the hangar. We boarded there for the eleven-hour overnight flight.

We landed at Al-Asad Airbase in western Iraq in complete darkness. The runways were entirely unlit, relying on the pilots' sophisticated equipment and their decades of combined experience to get us on the ground safely, which they executed flawlessly. We deplaned just after 7 p.m., with the Secret Service lighting our path with small flashlights. I vividly remember the darkness and the pervasive dust. It was Iraq—the desert—dry and rugged. And it was Christmas. I felt slightly fatigued, but I refused to let my spirits be dampened.

The element of surprise was our greatest ally as we arrived at the base. After meeting with the generals in a makeshift building, we entered the mess hall where the soldiers were gathered for their Christmas dinner, and anticipation filled the air. The troops, the very reason for our presence, soon recognized us and realized the special moment unfolding before them.

The initial surprise quickly gave way to whoops and cheers, followed by jubilant applause. Their warm welcome, their patriotism, and bravery were deeply stirring. I engaged in spontaneous interactions and captured many selfies. The soldiers' joy radiating from their beaming faces spoke volumes of their delight with our visit.

Next, we moved to a hangar to formally greet all of them. Before introducing the president, I expressed how honored I was to be there. "Thank you for your service, for your sacrifice, and for keeping us safe and free," I said. "I'm very proud of you. And, on behalf of our nation, I'm wishing you a merry Christmas and a happy and prosperous New Year. Thank you again, and to your families." Donald expressed his thoughts sincerely and genuinely: "We came to Al Asad to share our eternal gratitude for everything you do to keep America safe, strong, and free," he said. "Though you are thousands of miles away from your home and your loved ones, I hope you all had a merry Christmas. I also know that, speaking for your families, they are missing you and they love you. And you know they're every bit a part of your success; they make it possible. So they're very special to us, all of the families. It's because of your sacrifice that America's families can celebrate in safety and in peace. And we're doing great back at home."

Concluding his speech, Donald reiterated a point that is very important to him: "America is a peace-loving nation," he said. "But rest assured, if we are forced to fight, we will engage the enemy with overwhelming force like never before—like nobody has ever seen before. There is no military more capable, more lethal, more fearless, and more skilled than the United States Armed Forces. Nobody is even close. Our faith and confidence in you is absolute and total. You are the sentinels who watch over our nation. You are the warriors who defend our freedom. You are the patriots who ensure the flame of liberty burns forever bright. That's who you are. That's who you are. To everyone at Al-Asad Airbase, and every American serving overseas, may God bless you, may God protect you, and may God always keep you safe. We love you. We support you. We salute you. We cherish you. And together, we pray for justice, goodness, and peace on Earth."

Due to security concerns, our time on the ground was limited to just a few hours before we had to depart. Shortly after landing, we were back on Air Force One and headed back to Washington.

However, there was one more stop: At 2 a.m., we landed at Ramstein Air Base in Germany to refuel. There were troops there, too—so many men and women spending the holidays away from their families. The reception was just as warm as it had been in Iraq. The soldiers were elated to see us, lining up for pictures in the early hours of Christmas morning. But it was Donald and I who felt truly honored.

Less than twenty-four hours had passed since we'd left Washington. In the quiet of Air Force One, I reflected on all our travels that year—only our second in the White House. I had traveled on my own and accompanied my husband on numerous trips and meetings around the world. I'd spent time with brave children in hospitals, orphanages, and schools and had been welcomed by servicemen and -women at home, at sea, and now, in a war zone.

M

In May 2019, we traveled to Japan for our second official visit. Returning to a country for a second time brings a sense of familiarity, and this trip was no exception. Our relationship with Prime Minister Shinzo Abe and his lovely wife, Akie, had grown since our first visit and the occasions they spent with us in Washington and at Mar-a-Lago. Their invitation for another official visit was met with genuine enthusiasm. The United States and Japan enjoy close diplomatic and trade ties, so Donald had significant business to discuss with Prime Minister Abe. Additionally, he was to have the honor of being the first foreign leader to meet the new emperor, Naruhito, who had acceded to the throne earlier that month. It promised to be an exciting and momentous visit.

As First Lady, you meet many spouses and partners of foreign heads of state, but you form closer relationships with some than with others. Akie had an intriguing background—she'd been a radio DJ, run an organic bar in Tokyo, and attended a Catholic school, which is relatively rare in Japan. I formed a genuine connection with her, and this trip reaffirmed that link. While our husbands met to discuss official business, Akie and I explored the teamLab Borderless: Mori Building Digital Art Museum in central Tokyo. We were treated to an extraordinary spectacle: thirty children drawing sea creatures and then projecting them on the wall to create an enormous digital aquarium.

I was pleasantly surprised by the Be Best–inspired art the children had created in support of my initiative. It was so gratifying to see the acceptance of my program on a global scale. It was a beautiful blend of creativity and technology. Later, the four of us had the privilege of attending the Grand Sumo tournament at Ryōgoku Kokugikan Stadium in Tokyo. We had ringside seats. At the end of a match, Donald was invited into the ring. Wearing traditional ceremonial slippers, he made his way onto the dirt and presented the champion wrestler with a giant trophy. The crowd's ecstatic reaction was unforgettable, adding to the excitement of our visit.

Fortunately, during the pre-visit briefings, you can specify any dietary restrictions. For example, I made it known that I do not eat raw fish. However, I still made an effort to try local cuisine whenever possible. That night in Tokyo, the meal was a delicious blend of flavors and textures, showcasing the best of Japanese cuisine while accommodating my preferences. It was a memorable evening that encapsulated the warmth and hospitality of our hosts.

I was deeply shocked and saddened to hear of Mr. Abe's assassination in 2022. He was a remarkable leader, and the connection between him and Donald was genuine. The world would undoubtedly be a better place if more countries could foster such relationships.

Shortly after our return from Japan, we were off again to visit Her Majesty, Queen Elizabeth II. We'd met a year earlier over tea at Windsor Castle, where our conversation had extended far beyond the scheduled time. Her Majesty had graciously poured us tea and offered us scones with jam, while her cherished corgis lounged at her feet. We had truly connected and were delighted to have the opportunity to see her again.

The afternoon state visit at Buckingham Palace was truly unforgettable. Donald and I landed in Marine One on the perfectly manicured grounds and were greeted by Prince Charles and his wife, Camilla, the Duchess of Cornwall, who escorted us to the entrance where Her Majesty the Queen awaited. Amid the pomp of the ceremonial welcome by British guards, a sudden gust of wind ruffled my hat. I quickly grabbed at it to hold it in place and shared an unrestrained moment of laughter with the Queen and the Duchess. It was a lighthearted and spontaneous moment in an otherwise formal and dignified occasion.

Inside the resplendent palace, Her Majesty guided us through the royal collection, showcasing artifacts of profound significance to America.

The evening's state banquet was a formal and elegant affair. I was seated next to Prince Charles, and it was an absolute pleasure to reconnect with him. Our paths had crossed many years ago in New York City. This time we engaged in an interesting conversation about his deep-rooted commitment to environmental conservation.

The following night, Donald and I hosted an intimate dinner in honor of Prince Charles and the Duchess at the US ambassador's residence—a perfect expression of the enduring ties between our nations.

Despite the tumultuous backdrop of British politics at the time surrounding Brexit and changes at the Prime Minister's office, the Queen and her family extended a warm welcome to us, treating us with the utmost hospitality. Among the cherished gifts I received from Queen Elizabeth, one is particularly memorable to me: a specially commissioned silver box, with an enamel lid that features images of the rose, thistle, and shamrock, echoing the intricate ceiling motifs of Buckingham Palace's music room.

Our visit culminated with a moving ceremony commemorating the 75th anniversary of the D-Day landings in Normandy—a solemn tribute to the heroic sacrifices of British and American soldiers in the fight against the evil of the Nazis.

As we bid farewell to Her Majesty, we extended a cordial invitation for her return visit to the United States. She expressed her gratitude with a warm smile. Sadly, Her Majesty wasn't able to visit us again before her death in 2022, but our friendship with the Royal Family continues, and we exchange letters with King Charles to this day.

Chapter 15

Moments of Crisis

The First Lady's schedule is planned weeks, sometimes months in advance. It is a never-ending succession of White House events, speeches, rallies, trips, meetings, state visits, dinners, and luncheons. There is always a commitment to fulfill and a place to be. However, the role also demands readiness for unpredictable occurrences—natural disasters, terrorist attacks, tragedies, both large and small, that necessitate compassion and immediate action.

When Hurricane Harvey made landfall across the coasts of Texas and Louisiana on August 25, 2017, it devastated tens of thousands of lives, leaving many homeless. My husband and I recognized the urgency and knew we had to be there to help coordinate the response. Four days later, we were on our way to Texas on Air Force One, ready to offer our support and assistance to those in need.

Once on the ground in Texas, we met with local disaster relief teams and spoke with people whose lives had been upended by the storm. It was a deeply emotional experience for both of us. We encountered people who had lost their homes, their belongings, and, in some heartbreaking instances, their loved ones. We conferred with governors and mayors and collaborated closely with FEMA to guarantee that the affected communities received essential supplies—food, shelter, and water. Amid the chaos we witnessed, one encounter stands out starkly in my memory.

I served food to those in need, and later had the pleasure of meeting a thirty-five-year-old woman who had lost her home and everything she owned. I gave her a hug as we chatted. I reassured her that FEMA would provide the necessary assistance to help her rebuild her life. She had experienced such immense loss, and yet she radiated resilience and hope. She shared how her neighbors had come together, offering each other comfort and support. Her story was a poignant reminder of the strength and solidarity that can emerge from the depths of tragedy.

In moments like these, the role of the First Lady transcends formal duties. Her mission turns to fostering human connections, showing empathy, and offering support for those in need. The experiences and stories from these encounters remain vivid, shaping my perspective and reinforcing my dedication to serve others.

A little over a month later, on October 1, 2017, another tragic event unfolded: a mass shooting in Las Vegas. A sixty-four-year-old man unleashed a barrage of gunfire onto a music festival crowd from his perch on the thirtieth floor of a hotel. The sheer horror of the scene left us all in disbelief. The toll was devastating: sixty lives lost and hundreds more wounded.

I felt a profound need to be there—to support the injured and to grieve with the families of those who had been killed. Donald and I quickly began planning a visit to meet with first responders and those on the ground and also to visit the hospital where the victims were receiving treatment. It was important to us to personally connect with the victims and their families as they began their recovery process. I vividly recall our arrival at the hospital, where we had the privilege of meeting with the injured and their families in private. One young man, who had sustained a leg injury, tried to rise from his bed upon seeing us.

"Please don't stand up," I said, but he was determined.

"No, I want to stand up for you and the president. It's my honor," he insisted. The honor was mine—to be there with him and to let him know he'd be going home soon. Witnessing his and others' determination, courage, and strength only reinforced our dedication to stand by all of the victims during their journey to healing.

I would be reminded many times over my tenure as First Lady of the resilience of the American people.

M

My desire to help children, a deeply personal one I had made public through Be Best, would be tested two months after its launch. It was a moment that underscored the power and platform of the First Lady's office, a position that allowed me to amplify the voices of those who couldn't speak for themselves. Recent reports of families being separated at the US southern border had sparked widespread concern and condemnation. The children were apparently being held in overcrowded detention centers and in absolute squalor. This raised serious questions about their health and well-being. The lack of a clear plan for reuniting families and the absence of a definitive policy on these separations only added to the public's outrage.

I felt strongly that the situation demanded urgent attention and action to ensure the protection and reunification of these families.

My husband's hardline stance on immigration was well known—his campaign promise of building a wall between the United States and Mexico resonated with many. While I understood the importance of secure borders, I was blindsided by the reports in the media regarding the administration's immigration policies, particularly the separation of families and detention of children. I was never briefed and I had been completely unaware of the policy. As the First Lady, I felt it was imperative to get to the bottom of these allegations and understand the actions being taken by the White House. I immediately contacted my chief of staff to gather information and determine the appropriate action. It was critical to address this situation with speed, transparency, and compassion, ensuring that the policies reflected our values as a nation.

Occasional political disagreements between me and my husband were a part of our relationship, but I believed in addressing them privately rather than publicly challenging him. I found our discussions more productive when we could have a quiet dialogue at home, out of the public eye. Given my past experiences with unfair media narratives, I always approached the news with some skepticism. Before discussing the border crisis with him, I thoroughly educated myself on the situation.

I discovered that in April, Attorney General Jeff Sessions had announced a "zero tolerance" policy for those attempting to enter the United States illegally. This policy meant that individuals who would have previously been processed and released were now facing criminal charges and detention. As a result, families seeking asylum at legal ports of entry were now being separated under these new rules. Reports revealed thousands of children were separated from their parents and held in facilities surrounded by fences under the care of the U.S. Department of Health and Human Services.

I am sympathetic to all who wish to find a better life in this country. As an immigrant myself, I intimately understand the necessary if arduous process of legally becoming an American. While I support

strong borders, what was going on at the border was simply unacceptable and went against everything I believe in.

I immediately addressed my deep concerns with Donald regarding the family separations, emphasizing the trauma it was causing these
families. As a mother myself, I stressed:

"The government should not be taking children away from their
parents." I communicated with great clarity during that conversation:
"This has to stop." Donald assured me that he would investigate the
issue, and on June 20, he announced the end of the family separation
policy. An executive order was signed that afternoon, stating it was
"now the policy of this administration to maintain family unity, including by detaining alien families together where appropriate and
consistent with law and available resources."

This new policy was an important step, but I also needed to witness
the situation at the border firsthand. My presence could help maintain
pressure on officials to reunite families as quickly as possible. After discussing it with my husband, I received his support to go. I wanted to
show the American people how deeply we cared about this issue and
how dedicated we were to finding a solution. With the assistance of
the Secret Service and the Department of Homeland Security, a plan
was quickly put together for my trip to Texas the following day. There
was no formal announcement or detailed schedule—time was of the
essence. What truly mattered were the children at the border.

The following morning, on June 21, I traveled to McAllen, Texas,
a town just across the border from Reynosa, Mexico. It was one of
the epicenters of the border crisis. With Health and Human Services
Secretary Alex Azar, we visited the Upbring New Hope Children's
Center, operated by Lutheran Social Services of the South and supported by the federal government. It was one of many youth detention centers situated along the border in Texas. The center was

well-maintained, peaceful, and staffed by dedicated professionals, and I experienced a brief glimmer of hope during my visit. While most of the young people were teenagers who had arrived in the United States unaccompanied, there were still six children who had been separated from their families.

While interacting with the children, I asked about their well-being and learned about their experiences. Many of these children had been victims of exploitation by criminal organizations that used the children as drug mules. It quickly became evident to me that the root cause of their separation from their families was not the government but rather the dangerous influence of criminal cartels in their home countries. These children were innocent, frightened, and in need of reassurance. Their vulnerability strengthened my resolve to provide them with the care and support they deserved. I sought to offer comfort and encouragement to these young individuals, promising them that they would be looked after and protected. It was a reminder of the importance of our work in guaranteeing the safety and well-being of all children, especially those who have faced unimaginable hardships.

I had the opportunity to meet with the teachers, doctors, and staff at the center, where I expressed my willingness to learn and assist in any way I could. The program director shared with me that the children who came to the center often felt overwhelmed at first, but gradually relaxed as they became familiar with their surroundings and interacted with other children. I asked about the process of reuniting these children with their parents and was told that it is complex and challenging. Even with the best efforts of the staff and the well-maintained facilities, I knew that nothing could replace the love and care of a family.

Admittedly, there is a long, challenging road ahead, but I felt reassured that we were on the right path. Before departing, I asked my chief of staff about the possibility of returning soon. We began planning for another trip.

When I was initially preparing for my trip to the border, I was overcome with a sense of frustration towards the media's relentless spread of falsehoods and negativity. Their skewed narratives always seemed to divert attention away from the important issues at hand. I had seen this pattern countless times: An outlet would construct a story about me—a major distortion of the facts or even a complete fabrication with no basis in reality—and publish it. There would be no actual source, only an "anonymous source." These stories, fueled by the speed of the news cycle, quickly spread globally, perpetuating falsehoods that were difficult to correct. Social media allows these false narratives to snowball, gaining momentum and credibility they don't deserve.

I was determined, however, not to let the media's false narratives affect my mission to help the children and families at the border. In fact, I decided to let them know that their criticism would never stop me from doing what I feel is right. To make the point, I wore a particular jacket as I boarded the plane, a jacket that quickly became famous.

As the door on the plane closed, my press secretary's inbox was flooded with urgent emails from top-tier media outlets regarding the jacket I wore. The back of the jacket displayed a discreet yet impactful message: I REALLY DON'T CARE, DO YOU? "It's a message for the media," I said, "to let them know I was unconcerned with their opinions of me," I continued. She told me I couldn't say that. "Why not? It is the truth." I disagreed with her insistence that I couldn't say that. Ignoring my comments, she told a CNN reporter she was friendly with that it was simply a jacket, a fashion choice with no underlying message. I want to clarify that I never instructed her to provide misinformation. I believe it is crucial for accurate information to be relayed to the media in order to maintain transparency and credibility.

The media claimed the jacket meant I did not care about the children or the border, which was clearly not true. The jacket had nothing to do with the situation at the border or the children involved. I intentionally did not wear it during my visit to Texas, and only put it back on upon my return to DC. Unfortunately, the media's distorted reporting on the jacket overshadowed the importance of the children, the border, and the policy change. It was just another example of the media's irresponsible behavior.

M

A week later, I found myself once again at the border, this time in the state of Arizona. It was a heartbreaking situation, but one that I was determined to address. As First Lady, I saw the family separation issue as an extension of our important work with Be Best. Regardless of their background, every child deserves our support and protection. In the face of distractions and negative attention surrounding the jacket, I remained focused on the children.

I was committed to ensuring that changes were being made. I vowed not to rest until I was confident that progress was being made to protect these vulnerable children. Their well-being was my top priority, and I would stop at nothing to ensure they received the care and attention they deserved.

The Southwest Key migrant facility in Phoenix provided a safe and clean environment for the children I met during my visit. The staff went to great lengths to keep them occupied and cared for, but it was obvious that the children longed for the comfort and love of their parents. One particularly heartbreaking story I heard was of a young woman who had been a victim of violence on her journey to the border, only to give birth in the detention center. Another mother, just a teenager herself, tearfully shared her uncertainty about what the future held for her and her young son. These encounters left a lasting impact on me, reinforcing the importance of family unity and compassion in times of crisis.

M

It was a Saturday in October, a seemingly normal weekend, when my memories of 9/11 came flooding back. My husband was working, as he usually did. During weekends, the White House tends to be quieter compared to weekdays. While the atmosphere may not fully resemble a traditional weekend, our family appreciated the chance to enjoy the relative peace.

I was anticipating the visit of a close friend and his family, while Donald was preparing to go the West Wing. I was getting ready for my guests' arrival and not paying much attention to him. At some point, I noticed he hadn't left yet and was spending considerable time on the phone—talking to the generals, he said. He was unusually quiet that morning, and I sensed something significant was happening. Suddenly, he told me he was leaving: "I'm going to the Oval Office," he said. That was it. I had my own preparations to attend to, so I simply said, "Okay."

I was caught off guard when I received a call informing me that the president wanted to see me in the Oval Office. It was clear that something important was happening. I was ready to assist in any way possible, and quickly made my way downstairs to the Oval Office, but when I arrived, Donald wasn't there. Instead, I was directed to join him in the Situation Room—a first and unique experience for me. As I entered the Situation Room, I observed Donald in discussion with a group of generals. Someone offered me a seat next to him, and I gathered that the topic of conversation was the decision to pursue Abu Bakr al-Baghdadi, the Iraqi militant and so-called caliph of ISIS. It was clear that a plan of action was being formulated to apprehend one of the world's most dangerous terrorists.

"Watch this incredible action at work," Donald whispered to me.

The screens displayed real-time information of the unfolding situation. Curious about the specifics, I inquired about the number of troops involved, and the details were explained to me. My attention remained fixed on the black-and-white screens as a helicopter hovered above the ground, soldiers swiftly descending. The room was filled with a tense silence as everyone absorbed the incoming updates. Among the eight or nine individuals present, including myself, Donald, the vice president, National Security Advisor Robert O'Brien, Secretary of Defense Mark Esper, Chairman of the Joint Chiefs of Staff Mark Milley, and Deputy Director for Special Operations on the Joint Staff Brig. Gen. Marcus Evans, the atmosphere was one of anticipation. The mission to eliminate the leader of ISIS was a significant objective, and the successful completion of this operation would be a major accomplishment. This pivotal moment was one that Donald wanted to share with me.

I was deeply impressed by the bravery and skill of the special forces during the operation. Witnessing such precision and expertise was truly humbling. I excused myself before the mission was completed, understanding that my presence was not required and not wanting to disrupt their critical work. I am grateful to have had the opportunity to witness the incredible operation firsthand.

A special operations military working dog named Conan, a Belgian Malinois, played a crucial role in assisting members of Delta Force in tracking down al-Baghdadi through a tunnel during the raid. Sadly, he sustained some injuries. After his recovery, we were honored to welcome him to the White House to present him with a medal for his exceptional courage.

Chapter 16

2020

As Barron approached his fourteenth birthday, I was amazed at the remarkable young man he had become. Barron possesses a rare combination of intelligence, charm, and diligence. He had remained resolute in his character and values even through the whirlwind of changes and challenges that accompanied his father's election and presidency. He was navigating the spotlight with confidence and poise, embodying a maturity well beyond his years. With a circle of friends, a thirst for knowledge, and a range of hobbies, Barron continued to astound me with his growth and potential. My heart swelled with pride.

On June 18, 2019, we officially launched Donald's reelection campaign at the Amway Center in Orlando, Florida. The choice of location was strategic, as Florida had become our permanent home outside of Washington. As I introduced my husband once again for what promised to be another extraordinary run, memories of our first announcement at Trump Tower came flooding back.

"It has been my honor to serve as First Lady of this incredible country for the past two years," I said, the stadium quieting. "I'm excited to do it for six more. I'm proud of all that my husband, this administration, and our entire family have done on behalf of the American people in such a short time. He truly loves this country and will continue to work on your behalf as long as he can. All of us will." The applause was thunderous. "And now, I want to introduce my husband, the president of the United States, Donald J. Trump."

"USA! USA! USA!" the audience cheered.

"Our country is now thriving," Donald said. "Our economy is the envy of the world, perhaps the greatest economy we've ever had in the history of our country. We accomplished more than any other president has in the first two and half years of a presidency and under circumstances that no president has had to deal with."

That last part was indisputably true. Those circumstances Donald spoke of were opposition within the Republican Party, resistance from the Democrats, and relentless criticism from the media. Add to that a special counsel investigation, smear campaigns, anonymous sources, fake news, sham investigations, and, of course, impeachment.

On December 18, 2019, the House of Representatives had finally taken the anticipated step of adopting two articles of impeachment against my husband: abuse of power and obstruction of Congress. To be quite honest, I was surprised that it had taken them so long to make their move. While there was absolutely no truth to the allegations, it had been abundantly clear from the very beginning that the Democrats were hell-bent on pursuing impeachment. Their relentless cries for Donald's removal since the day of his election had merely been a prelude to this inevitable outcome. The hearings, the inquiries, and the committee votes were more than a grand political spectacle designed to tarnish his presidency. I am convinced that, if he were to be reelected, they would undoubtedly attempt to impeach him once again. It was all a futile attempt to hinder his leadership and undermine his authority.

Throughout all of these attempts to derail his presidency, Donald stood up for his convictions and reiterated his commitment to serving the American people. And then, an unforeseen circumstance drastically transformed the global landscape.

M

In December 2019, I first saw news reports from China about a "novel coronavirus." There was no talk then of it spreading beyond China, let alone becoming a global pandemic. No one could foresee the future, but the unease in the air was concerning, and the lack of real information troubled me deeply.

The first case of COVID-19 in the United States was reported on January 21, stemming from a traveler from China. In response, a White House coronavirus task force was quickly established. Suddenly, events were unfolding at lightning speed, and Donald was on top of all of it. He declared a public health emergency on January 31, and three days later, before there was a single coronavirus death in the United States, announced a ban on travel from China to the United States. For foreign nationals who had recently been in China, this meant no entry into the country. For Americans, it meant a fourteen-day quarantine. This travel ban almost certainly saved countless American lives. In the midst of a highly politicized atmosphere, my husband's actions were unfairly attacked, but history will remember his swift and necessary decisions as crucial in safeguarding the health and safety of our nation.

My calendar was packed, filled with events scheduled months in advance, but I was fully committed to fulfilling all of my obligations. The campaign was in full swing, and I had important engagements planned, including Barron's birthday in March, a trip to Oklahoma, and the Easter Egg Roll in April. Additionally, an official visit to India to meet with prime minister Narendra Modi was on our schedule.

In the meantime, the impeachment proceedings moved forward. They began with a full House vote followed by the submission of articles to the Senate on January 16. However, they lacked substance, as no witnesses were called, and no documents were subpoenaed during the supposed trial. It became clear that the trial was merely a performance and a distraction, both for the American people and for Donald. The constant impeachment chatter had become background noise, something I had grown accustomed to. It was evident not just to me and Donald, but to most of America, that the process was not genuine.

A day after Donald delivered his third State of the Union address, during which a handful of Democrats rudely got up and walked out, the Senate voted. While all Democrats voted to convict, the majority of Republicans voted in favor of acquittal, resulting in my husband being cleared of the charges.

On February 6, the day after the impeachment trial ended, I left the East Room press conference and entered the Oval Office, where I took a seat next to my husband at the Resolute desk. I was there for a briefing on Covid and our upcoming India trip, which was now just two weeks away.

Back in September, Donald had hosted Prime Minister Modi in Houston, Texas, at a "Howdy Modi" rally. An astonishing fifty thousand people had shown up, many of them Indian Americans. Not long after, Prime Minister Modi extended the invitation to the president and me for a two-day state visit and to celebrate the rebuilding of the largest cricket stadium in the world, located in Modi's home state of Gujarat. We graciously accepted his invitation.

Given the rapid spread of the virus, I was reluctant to travel to India at that time. It was important to prioritize the safety and well-being of our team and adhere to the warnings and guidelines issued by public health organizations. Additionally, it was crucial to consider the message that our travel might convey to the public, especially in light of the prevailing travel restrictions and advisories for the general population. It was essential to act responsibly and in alignment with current guidelines to avoid any misinterpretations.

For international trips, an advance team travels ahead to prepare everything on the ground. Given the spread of the virus, I needed assurance that it was safe for them to travel. Although our visit would only last two days, the advance team would be on the ground for two weeks.

Sitting across from me in the Oval Office were Dr. Anthony Fauci from the National Institute of Health, Dr. Robert Redfield from the CDC, and HHS Secretary Alex Azar.

"How safe is it to travel to India at this time?" I asked, looking at Dr. Fauci. "How many cases do they have?" I was curious.

"Not many," he said. "Only three."

This seemed utterly impossible. I had announced that my advance team would depart for India in a mere two days, but the uncertainty surrounding the number and severity of cases gave me pause. The risk was undeniable, and as the weight of responsibility for my team settled heavily on my shoulders, the room fell into a hushed stillness. I cast a brief glance toward my trusted physician standing at the back of the room, silently conveying my decision with a solemn shake of my head.

"Perhaps we should cancel the trip," I said. Their incredulous gazes made it clear that this was not a welcome suggestion. In spite of the logistical challenges and diplomatic implications, I could not ignore the well-being of my team. Their health and safety were of utmost importance—they were not just valuable assets, but individuals with families and loved ones counting on them. Merely assuring them with, "Everything is fine. Don't worry," was not sufficient in my eyes.

Dr. Fauci and his team confidently assured us that, given the information available, our trip was indeed safe to undertake. After some deliberation, Donald ultimately decided that we would go.

The advance team departed two days later, and we followed on February 24. The buzz of the virus was unavoidable, dominating every conversation. Our journey was brief yet enchanting: We began with a rally at the grand Motera Stadium, attended by a staggering 100,000 fervent spectators. "India shall forever hold a cherished place in our hearts," Donald declared, eliciting thunderous applause. We then flew to Agra for a private tour of the majestic Taj Mahal, followed by a sumptuous state banquet in New Delhi. The following day, I had the privilege of visiting the Sarvodaya Vidyalaya Senior Secondary School, where I engaged with students and educators to gain insight into their exclusive "Happiness Classes," aimed at alleviating stress. We received such a colorful and warm welcome in India, and I was pleased that everything went according to plan.

M

In hindsight, we were fortunate that no one fell ill with COVID-19 during our time abroad. As February drew to a close, it became evident that the virus would pose a more significant threat than initially thought. The uncertainty surrounding the situation was daunting, and we found ourselves constantly reassessing our plans in light of new information. The rapidly evolving nature of the pandemic meant that the world was on the brink of significant change, with unforeseen consequences. Little did I anticipate that our journey to India would mark the final international trip of my husband's term.

There were conflicting opinions among experts on the best safety protocols for our nation, so I took it upon myself to implement changes within the residence and the Office of the First Lady. I directed my staff to work remotely whenever possible, to maintain a safe distance when in the office, and to wear face masks in adherence to the latest guidelines. I made sure to wear a mask and diligently sanitize high-touch surfaces.

I made the difficult decision to suspend public tours of the White House, a beloved tradition, in the interest of safety amid the spread of the virus. Furthermore, I directed most of the residence staff to remain at home to prioritize their well-being. Donald, Barron, and I would manage with a reduced team.

The East Wing was also closed, with all staff working remotely. Those who needed to come in had to undergo COVID-19 testing first. My last in-person event was the National PTA Legislative Conference in Virginia on March 10.

Donald's focus on tracking the spread of the virus and coordinating resources was essential to supporting our healthcare system. By uniting individuals from various sectors, he effectively mobilized efforts to address the growing demands for ventilators, tests, and personnel. Along with the rest of my team, I remained committed to our mission of caring for our families and supporting those on the front lines.

The pervasive fear and uncertainty among people worldwide deeply affected me, prompting me to offer information, support, and a sense of calm whenever possible.

On March 19, I released the first in a series of public service announcements on my official Twitter account. "While changes need to be made now," I said, "this is not how we will live forever." I wanted to assure the public that we were actively listening and diligently working to gather and share information to the best of our abilities here at the White House. I would follow that first announcement with many more over the coming months, shared on my social media and broadcast nationally on television, as I coordinated phone calls with my counterparts in countries such as France, Japan, Canada, Germany, and Italy to exchange insights and offer mutual support. In addition to offering words of support and guidance through PSAs, I organized boxes of Be Best supplies and food from the White House garden for hospitals, foster care homes, and shelters. And we delivered lunches to local fire stations for firefighters and first responders, as well as to a home for single mothers.

In a PSA released on April 9, I recommended wearing a mask when meeting with other people to help prevent the spread of respiratory droplets and expressed deep gratitude to the true heroes of our time—nurses, doctors, and teachers.

Amid the chaos, a sense of solidarity emerged, showcasing the limitless strength and courage of our nation. Witnessing individuals selflessly put their lives on hold to aid and protect others was truly inspiring. It was during this challenging time that we saw the remarkable spirit of unity and compassion that defines us as a nation.

M

As the global pandemic spread, the United States also faced a crucial election year. The importance of leadership and stability during such challenging times could not be overstated. With many Americans looking to Donald for guidance and support, the upcoming election held immense significance.

On May 26, a pivotal incident unfolded as a nine-minute video circulated on social media—a cell phone recording showing the killing of a Black Minneapolis resident by a white police officer. Within a mere two days, the video had gone viral, serving as the spark that ignited a national conversation on police brutality and racial injustice.

In the aftermath of his tragic death, the firing of all four officers involved in his arrest did not quell the public outcry for justice. Instead, protests demanding accountability and systemic reforms to address police brutality intensified across the nation.

However, this tragic incident did not warrant dismantling the entire system. I've long championed the right to peaceful protest as a cornerstone of American democracy, but the widespread violence and destruction we witnessed were troubling.

Additionally, the disregard for public health guidelines amid the COVID-19 pandemic was worrisome, especially coming from those who had previously advocated for strict measures.

The violent demonstrations in cities across the country, driven by the inflammatory rhetoric of Black Lives Matter leaders, caused widespread destruction and harm to businesses and communities. The deployment of the National Guard to several cities by May 31 highlighted the seriousness of the situation. I couldn't help but wonder what can be gained from such destructive behavior, as it only leads to more suffering and devastation. Our country has a proud history of seeking peaceful and constructive ways to address issues and make positive change.

From the White House, I observed protesters on the North Lawn, their anger and hostility tangible and escalating.

On Friday morning, I issued a statement: "Our country allows for peaceful protest, but there is no reason for violence. I've seen our citizens unify & take care of one another through COVID-19 & we can't stop now." I shared this message on my social media platforms, hoping to appeal to reason and restraint. But I'm afraid my words fell on deaf ears.

On the afternoon of May 29, I was in the residence, on the south side of the White House. When I walked over to the north side, where the dining room and Barron's room were located, I could clearly see and hear the protesters gathering outside. Their chants and shouts were loud, indicating a sizable crowd had gathered on Lafayette Street, but this was not a regular occurrence that I frequently witnessed directly and via television updates. There was little I could directly influence, so I attempted to continue with my daily routine.

Suddenly, the situation outside the White House took a concerning turn as protesters became more assertive and attempted to breach the gates on the east and west sides of the building. Their demands to see the president, who was in the Oval Office on the ground floor, indicated a desire to disrupt and sow chaos rather than peacefully exercise their First Amendment rights. This level of aggression and insistence on accessing the president's office was highly unusual and alarming. The air crackled with tension; a rare and unsettling sight was unfolding before our eyes.

While I wasn't worried for my safety or that of my family— knowing that the Secret Service and law enforcement were vigilant and capable —I couldn't completely dismiss the unpredictability of the situation. I spent part of that afternoon with Barron and my parents as the intensity mounted, but there was little I could do.

Returning to my office on the second floor of the residence, I resumed work only to be interrupted by a loud knock on my door. The thick White House doors muffled little, and the assertive tone of the Secret Service agent's voice left no doubt about the urgency: "Ma'am, we need to leave the residence. We need to go to the bunker. The president is on his way there already."

"Really?" I was genuinely taken aback. I expressed reluctance, saying that I was sure we were safe on the second floor. The residence staff had already been evacuated. I simply couldn't fathom the possibility of anyone breaching the building, let alone reaching the residence on the second floor. I asked again, "Do we need to go?"

"Yes, ma'am," he replied with no hesitation.

Annoyed, I gathered my jacket, along with both my personal and White House phones, slipped on my shoes, and headed to get Barron and my parents, only to find them already waiting for me at the elevator.

While I understood the precaution for the president's safety, evacuating all of us seemed an excessive measure from my perspective. Nevertheless, the Secret Service had made its decision, and it was pointless to contest it.

Once before, when aircraft flew over the White House, the Secret Service had put us on standby, although no further action was required. That experience had prepared me somewhat to always be ready for an emergency, but I had never anticipated needing to use the bunker to seek refuge from a crowd of aggrieved protesters.

Donald was already in the bunker when we arrived, and he could sense my frustration. He remained composed; as president, he understood the Secret Service's responsibility to make swift, challenging security decisions, which he never disregarded. "They wanted all of us here," he said.

Outside, the situation appeared to worsen. Rioters hurled bottles and bricks, injuring agents. People were being arrested. We eagerly anticipated returning upstairs to resume our work, but we were required to wait for clearance from the Secret Service. I had brought my phones in the hopes of accomplishing some work, but found, to my disappointment, that they did not function so deep underground. So, we patiently waited.

After approximately two hours, Secret Service and law enforcement had brought the situation under control enough for us to be escorted back upstairs. Once back in the residence, I realized that I still had no phone signal, and neither did anyone in my family. When I asked, the Secret Service informed me that all phones become permanently inoperative once inside the bunker, as part of a security protocol.

That first week of protests prompted me to reflect deeply. This was our fourth year in the White House, and my desire to see the country heal had never been stronger. I craved a harmonious existence, where peace, prosperity, and shared triumphs were the norm. Where people collaborated toward common aspirations: enhanced education, heightened safety for our children, and improved lives for all Americans.

Seeing BLACK LIVES MATTER painted in monumental letters on 16th Street NW in D.C. and Fifth Avenue in front of Trump Tower in New York made me ponder the ultimate impact of slogans, protests, and historical monuments in shaping our society. While racial unrest may prompt the removal of certain statues, it is imperative that we do not simply erase the less favorable aspects of our past. Rather, we must use these moments as opportunities for education and growth, ensuring that future generations understand the complexities of history and work toward a more inclusive and just society. Simply erasing the disagreeable parts of the past cannot be the answer. We must instead learn from every facet of our history—to avoid it repeating itself. Nonetheless, I maintained my hope and optimism.

The United States, a true melting pot of races, religions, and ethnicities, inevitably harbors potential for conflict among those diverse groups if we don't learn to respect and accept people for who they are as individuals, beyond their group identities. Peaceful disagreement—devoid of violence, which accomplishes nothing—should be our shared goal. Yet the focus on grouping people often leads to stereotyping and labels, fostering intolerance. We face daunting challenges that demand earnest effort, beginning with genuine respect for each other's individuality—not with anger, violence, and resentment toward entire groups of people we barely know.

Our differences create a more fascinating, creative, and innovative world.

Today, some groups attempt to impose their ideologies on everyone, deepening the divisions in our society. One example is the ongoing debate over trans inclusion in sports, specifically when male-born athletes who identify as female compete against women. Male bodies generally have physical advantages—muscle strength, height, bone density, and lung capacity—that can affect fairness in competition, even at the high school level.

Some argue that the number of trans-athletes is low, but even one can upset the balance in a female league or tournament due to these physical advantages. High school athletes often dedicate years to training with the hope of being recruited by universities. Seeing that dream collapse is an unnecessary and avoidable consequence.

This issue also has broader implications, including the loss of future earning potential as professional athletes and a potential setback for equal pay in sports.

As many of you may know, I fully support the LGBTQIA+ community. But we must also ensure that our female athletes are protected and respected. It's time for our polarized communities to come together, return to the center, and rediscover respect and tolerance for diverse thoughts and beliefs.

The people had entrusted my husband with leadership, and I took great pride in the progress we had achieved. It was a tumultuous summer, yet our resolve remained steadfast to pursue another term. While Election Day outcomes are unpredictable, we were determined to see through the initiatives we had set in motion.

Navigating through formidable opposition and crises, my husband's presidency proved to be one of the most challenging in recent memory. True to his promise, he'd disrupted the political establishment, giving voters the change they had asked for. We hoped they would give us the opportunity to accomplish even more.

M

With the election now only a month away, on October 1, Donald and I tested positive for COVID-19. Throughout the pandemic, I had been meticulous about disinfecting door handles and remote controls, consistently wearing a mask, practicing social distancing, and isolating as much as possible. Regardless of where I contracted it, we now faced the reality of the illness.

I was not overly concerned for myself, but my worry for Donald, and for my parents and Barron, was overwhelming. Barron and I had spent the previous evening chatting in my room, and although he continued to test negative, I feared he might soon fall ill as well. He was young and healthy, but the uncertainties surrounding the virus were daunting. As any mother would, I worried deeply about my son.

Initially, I experienced no symptoms, but when they hit, they all hit at once. It felt like a severe flu: fatigue, fever, body aches, a cough, and headaches. It was uncomfortable, but never alarming. Donald's symptoms were more severe. After his positive test, his doctors monitored him closely in the residence. He insisted that he felt fine, but I could tell, as any wife can, that he was not feeling well.

That first night, I vigilantly checked his breathing as he lay in bed, monitored his oximeter, and felt his forehead. In the middle of the night, I thought he was improving, but by morning, his condition had clearly worsened. During our consultation with the doctors,

I suggested he go to Walter Reed National Military Medical Center. Predictably, Donald resisted; he wanted to remain at the White House and continue working, even though he was ill.

From my perspective, there was no reason for him *not* to go to the hospital. He could work just as efficiently from there as from the residence, and his medical team could provide round-the-clock care, including the best available treatments.

I explained, "You have a fever. You need to go to Walter Reed. There is an entire team there that can monitor you. You can't stay here another night. What if you suddenly get worse? I'm not a doctor." The doctors concurred, advising, "Mr. President, we agree with the First Lady. You better go to Walter Reed." We were uncertain how quickly he would recover or how severe his condition might become.

He flew to Walter Reed on Friday afternoon. Fortunately, under the care of the incredible doctors there, Donald recovered swiftly. He returned home two days later, and soon resumed his presidential and campaign activities. With the election less than a month away, Donald was eager to continue sharing his message. I decided to forgo the aggressive treatments that were administered to Donald and focused on maintaining my health with milder drugs, vitamins, and a nutritious diet. Still, the virus persisted in my system for a couple of weeks. During this time, Barron also tested positive, but fortunately, he did not experience any strong symptoms.

While Donald was actively campaigning, I focused on my family, continued my work on the Be Best initiative, and oversaw the completion of the tennis pavilion and the Rose Garden.

M

Going into November, I did not know if Donald would win the election. In elections as close as this, it's difficult to say. Donald had a strong record he could point to, an incredible list of accomplishments, and even more support from the American people. But the media, Big Tech, and the deep state were all determined to prevent Donald's re-election, by any means necessary.

I was mentally prepared for life as a private citizen again, and I had no doubt it would be as rewarding as before. But I couldn't help thinking of all we could achieve with another four years. There was so much more we could do, more social issues to tackle, more restoration projects to take on, and more ways of inspiring Americans and people worldwide. It's a difficult job, and you're never done, but I felt privileged to do it. Everyone was working very hard for another term.

In some ways, everything felt more manageable this time. We had been through it all before. We knew what to expect. And so much had changed in the last four years. Our lives were completely different. We were already in the White House. Barron was much older. The 2020 election felt so much less like a question mark. I may not have been able to predict the winner, but I went into the election incredibly optimistic. I could see how much support Donald had across the country.

Still, we faced substantial challenges, many resulting from the pandemic and an even more polarized landscape than had existed in 2016. The media constantly circulated stories that blamed Donald for what the country was going through simply because he didn't wear a mask. But he was doing everything he could to protect Americans.

The mainstream media doubled down on its campaign of hate and lies against my husband. They peddled all sorts of false stories, from the Russia hoax to Ukraine, stories that were endlessly promoted on social media. At the same time, the media seemed strangely uninterested in covering news that could harm the opposition's campaign at all. Even more outrageous, the media latched on to a story in which fifty-one intelligence officials supposedly agreed that the former vice president's son's laptop from Hell investigation was part of some sort of Russian disinformation campaign. (A subsequent congressional investigation showed that his campaign actively recruited officials to sign on to this preposterous claim, as a way to prevent the American people from learning the truth.) In fact, Media Research Center found that 94 percent of the evening news coverage of my husband on ABC, NBC, and CBS was negative. It seemed nearly impossible to find a positive story about Donald's presidency, despite the incredible achievements of his administration. With all these enemies aligned, I worried the election would be unfair.

The day before the election, I traveled to North Carolina to give a speech and then returned to Palm Beach. On the morning of November 3rd, I voted and headed back to Washington. The original plan for election night was to hold a gathering (and party, hopefully) at the Trump International Hotel in D.C., but the city government's COVID-19 regulations would not allow it. Someone came up with the idea of an Election Night Victory Party at the White House, so the White House it was.

On election night, I watched TV in my room with Barron. Donald would come in, watch with us, and then go to answer some phone call. I was very calm and stoic, the same as I was on the election night in 2016. I knew the outcome was out of my control. I wouldn't let myself become too anxious or obsessed. Donald enjoyed early wins in Kentucky, West Virginia, and South Carolina, followed by Alabama, Mississippi, Oklahoma, and Arkansas. But then, at 11:30 pm, Fox News projected that Arizona would flip to Biden. I couldn't believe it. How could they call it so early before all the votes were counted? It was another sign that this was not a normal election. Soon, the media reported that due to the way different states counted mail-in ballots and the various mail-in deadlines, the results would not be clear for several days. At this point, everything was called into question for me. An election should be held on a single day, and polls should close at midnight. Votes are counted, and that's it. We need that certainty. That's how fair elections should be done. You can't continue to count votes for days, which is what they did. It was a mess. Many Americans still have doubts about the election to this day. I am not the only person who questions the results.

It was a late night. At 2:30 in the morning, we went down to the East Room. Donald made remarks on the status of the election. "I want to thank the American people for their tremendous support. Millions and millions of people voted for us tonight. And a very sad group of people is trying to disenfranchise that group of people, and we won't stand for it," he said.

We stopped at the Map Room, which was set up as a command center with computers and teams of people discussing the election. It was around 3:30 am when I said goodnight to the team and went to sleep.

The uncertainty dragged on for several more days, with suspicious voting activity being reported all across the country. It was November 7, three and a half days after the election, before the final results were called. It was over.

It was disappointing, of course. Not only because of Donald and his supporters' hard work but also because of all we had hoped to accomplish in a second term. And because we knew how the country would change, how much of Donald's good work would be undone by the next administration.

After the election, I focused myself on the practical tasks needing my attention. I began preparing for our impending move to Mar-a-Lago and started research to find a new school for Barron in Palm Beach.

As with all First Ladies who preceded me, it was my obligation to record the contents of the White House's historic rooms, including taking archival photographs of all the renovations. Several months in advance, I organized a qualified team of photographers, archivists, and designers to work with me in the White House to ensure perfect execution. As required, we scheduled January 6, 2021, to complete the work on behalf of our nation. This is a very significant undertaking and requires great care, attention to detail, and concentration—both in the planning and execution. At the time, I wasn't thinking about it as the day Congress would certify the election results.

On January 6, I gathered with my team early in the morning to get started on our archival work. At one point, I glanced out the sunroom window, one of the highest vantage points in the White House and noticed a sizeable gathering of people below. Though aware of activity outside, my attention remained on our tasks. We later moved between floors, engrossed in discussions about our ongoing projects, away from any television screens. Donald was occupied with his responsibilities, and I with mine: to document everything quickly because I knew we would leave the White House soon.

At 2:25 p.m., I received a text from my press secretary, who was not present in the White House; I don't know if she was even in D.C. I glanced at her text. She was asking if I wanted to "denounce the violence." I found the question perplexing—when had I ever condoned violence? Throughout my tenure, I consistently denounced violence on numerous occasions. However, at that moment, my team was already behind the schedule and focused on the task. I wasn't aware of the events unfolding at the Capitol building. Traditionally, the First Lady's chief of staff provides detailed briefings surrounding our nation's important issues. My second White House chief of staff failed to do so. Had I been fully informed of all the details, naturally, I would have immediately denounced the violence that occurred at the Capitol Building. I have always and will always condemn violence.

Upon receiving information from the Chief Usher regarding the situation at the Capitol, I told my team to collect their equipment and return home. I was worried for their safety.

Once in my room, I turned on the TV. The news coverage was shocking; the violence we witnessed was unequivocally unacceptable. While I recognized that many individuals felt the election was mishandled and that the vice president should halt the confirmation process, we must never resort to violence.

Chapter 17

Fostering the Future

One chapter ends, and another begins. On January 20, 2021, Donald and I rose early, prepared ourselves, and made our way to the Diplomatic Room, where we bid farewell to our staff. Emotions ran high—our time at the White House had been transformative, forging deep bonds with many.

After our heartfelt farewells, we walked across the South Lawn to Marine One, taking in the moment's significance. Gratitude filled me for the incredible opportunity I'd been given. And I reminded myself that no matter what lay ahead, I would navigate it with resilience and grace. Boarding Marine One, we flew to Joint Base Andrews where we held a brief ceremony. From there, Air Force One carried us one last time as President and First Lady, landing in Palm Beach, Florida, before noon. A motorcade escorted us to Mar-a-Lago, where suddenly, I found myself a private citizen again.

I took a deep breath and allowed myself a brief moment to let this new reality sink in. For four years, I had been humbled—daily—by the opportunity to serve our country. Becoming First Lady of the United States had been the greatest honor of my life, and while I had hoped for another four years, I understood that that part of my life was ending. Nevertheless, I took comfort in the knowledge that my work did not have to stop simply because I was no longer in the White House. It *couldn't* stop. We had made astonishing progress, but there was still so much to do. Within a few minutes of being home, I realized, I was already looking ahead to the future—the brighter, safer, more peaceful future.

M

Not long after becoming a private citizen again, I started working on developing a strategy that would allow me to move away from the more policy- and awareness-driven work I was doing as First Lady—meaningful, important work, to be sure—to the kind of action-oriented initiatives I could execute more effectively outside of my role in the White House. In particular, I wanted to focus my efforts on the foster care community, a cause that had become increasingly important to me over my last years as First Lady.

I had learned from speaking to experts as well as former foster children that many in the foster care community lack the support and stability to finish their education and gain meaningful employment. According to the National Foster Youth Institute, only 50 percent of foster children finish high school, and only 3 percent of former foster children obtain a college degree. Twenty percent of the children in foster care will become homeless after aging out of the system, and only half will have gainful employment by the age of twenty-four.

These statistics were sobering and disheartening, but I quickly sensed a way in which I could make tangible changes in the lives of some of these kids. Continuing the work I had begun as First Lady, I launched Fostering the Future, a Be Best initiative aimed at supporting children in the foster care system. The program provides access to tech-focused university education through scholarships awarded to foster children. Scholarship recipients would learn in a supportive environment and gain the knowledge and skills to secure meaningful and stable jobs in the technology sector. Access to a computer science education would prepare these young people to enter the workforce and ultimately reach financial independence. By supporting education and career development, Fostering the Future offers a sustainable foundation for a brighter future. Currently, a number of young people from the foster community are enrolled in universities as a result of this initiative. As an initiative focused on technology education, it seemed fitting that funding for Fostering the Future would come, primarily, through my involvement with blockchain technologies. Understanding that there was a need for a decentralized platform that would allow for direct engagement with my fans, free from the constraints of major tech corporations I along with a team of experts developed two blockchain verticals, targeted to my audience, that provided everything from supply and design to production, marketing, sales, and delivery: Melaniatrump.com and USAmemorabilia.com. The driving force behind working with blockchain technology is autonomy. Blockchain provides a solution that protects me from being deplatformed from third party technology companies that don't like my name or my politics.

I take pride in our proactive adoption of blockchain technologies, which includes initiatives like a special airdrop we initiated during Christmas 2022, using blockchain technology to deliver a limited-edition animated Christmas ornament to customers who had previously purchased our digital collectibles. Our innovative approach has positioned us as pioneers in this space, inspiring others to follow our lead. Since my departure from the White House, I have created an array of digital collectibles, Christmas ornaments, and jewelry, using block-chain technology. My collaborations with Navy SEALs, celebrations of national holidays, and features on America's national parks have been a powerful business venture, while also supporting the Fostering the Future initiative.

M

After establishing Fostering the Future, my Executive Senior Advisor Marc Beckman and I pursued partnerships with schools and universities to channel donations for scholarships benefiting foster care children. We were thrilled to secure our first partnership with a leading tech-education company. A few months after signing the contract, however, the school withdrew from the partnership when its board decided against any affiliation with me. Despite my efforts to focus solely on children's education and my willingness to avoid any public association with the program, the school remained firm and terminated the agreement.

It has been troubling to witness people who claim to care about the well-being of communities engage in actions that harm those communities. This trend is not only prevalent but appears to be escalating unchecked.

The "cancel mob" now includes corporations, traditional media, influential social media figures, and cultural institutions. This disheartening trend reflects the current socio-political landscape in the United States. These ideologues, often lacking basic decency, can cause collateral damage to innocent people. It is evident that these self-proclaimed "activists" show little regard for the consequences of their behavior, even when it adversely impacts the people they purport to care about.

Here are just a few examples from my own experience. I was invited to be the featured guest speaker at a fundraiser for children in foster care. In the months leading up to the event, the organizer and their family, including several elderly employees, faced harassment from the *New York Times* and social media activists. This created an atmosphere of fear, leading local government officials to take unnecessary measures, such as fingerprinting those involved. Ultimately, the event never happened due to this pressure, leaving foster care children as the primary victims.

I was shocked and dismayed to learn that my long-time bank decided to terminate my account and deny my son the opportunity to open a new one. This decision appeared to be rooted in political discrimination, raising serious concerns about civil rights violations. It is troubling to see financial services withheld based on political affiliation.

A month later, after lengthy negotiations, the CEO of a multinational investment bank decided to terminate discussions about a proposed "Melania Trump Technology" Special Purpose Acquisition Company. While the senior management team recognized the mutual commercial potential, they were unable to proceed without the CEO's endorsement.

After leaving the White House, I had an experience in the media sector that highlights the venom of cancel culture. Following a year of collaboration and a signed contract, my media partner was acquired by a private equity firm. The new leadership chose not to honor our agreement due to personal animosity towards my husband. There was the potential for a breach of contract lawsuit, but the CEO upheld their decision, demonstrating a troubling disregard for professional integrity. The time and effort invested in this media initiative was ultimately compromised due to political biases. However, my Executive Senior Advisor has re-entered the marketplace, securing more suitable partners and restarting the process. Regrettably, all previous work on the project has been rendered ineffective.

Recently, our contract with a prominent email distribution service provider was abruptly cancelled without notice or explanation. This forced us to reevaluate our processes, and we have since taken the initiative to manage our email distribution internally.

The cancellation continues—an attitude by businesses both big and small that never ceases to surprise me. It is ironic that my business acumen is criticized, while other former government officials receive praise for similar endeavors, such as securing multimillion-dollar media deals. This disparity can only be explained by biases related to my last name and political affiliation.

As we were soon to learn, cancel culture in America extends far beyond social media and the corporate sector.

M

Living my life with a core set of principles provides me with a foundation that leads to consistent and rational decision-making.

Individual liberty exists at the heart of my core principles and as such, always remains bedrock. Unequivocally, there is no room for negotiation when it comes to this fundamental right that we all are born with: individual liberty. Personal Freedom.

I have always believed it is critical for people to take care of themselves first. It's a very straightforward concept; in fact, we are all born with a set of fundamental rights, including the right to enjoy our lives. We are all entitled to maintain a gratifying and dignified existence.

This common-sense approach applies to a woman's natural right to make decisions about her own body and health. When one is physically and mentally strong, she can elevate her loved ones, family members, friends, and business colleagues.

It is imperative to guarantee that women have autonomy in deciding their preference of having children, based on their own convictions, free from any intervention or pressure from the government. Why should anyone other than the woman herself have the power to determine what she does with her own body?

A woman's fundamental right of individual liberty, to her own life, grants her the authority to terminate her pregnancy if she wishes. Restricting a woman's right to choose whether to terminate an unwanted pregnancy is the same as denying her control over her own body. I have carried this belief with me throughout my entire adult life.

There are several legitimate reasons for a woman to choose to have an abortion. For instance, if her life is at risk, rape, a congenital birth defect, plus severe medical conditions. Indeed, most people agree that abortion should be permissible in cases where a woman's life is at risk due to the pregnancy, as well as those situations where the pregnancy is a result of rape or incest.

Timing matters.

It is important to note that historically, most abortions conducted during the later stages of pregnancy were the result of severe fetal abnormalities that probably would have led to the death or stillbirth of the child. Perhaps even the death of the mother. These cases were extremely rare and typically occurred after several consultations between the woman and her doctor. As a community, we should embrace these common-sense standards. Again, timing matters.

Additionally, many women opt for abortions due to personal medical concerns. These situations with significant moral implications weigh heavily on the woman and her family and deserve our empathy.

Consider, for example, the complexity inherent in the decision of whether the mother should risk her own life to give birth.

When confronted with an unexpected pregnancy, young women frequently experience feelings of isolation and significant stress. I, like most Americans, am in favor of the requirement that juveniles obtain parental consent before undergoing an abortion. I realize this may not always be possible. Our next generation must be provided with knowledge, security, safety, and solace, and the cultural stigma associated with abortion must be lifted.

The slogan "My Body, My Choice" is typically associated with women activists and those who align with the pro-choice side of the debate.

But if you really think about it, "My Body, My Choice" applies to both sides—a woman's right to make an independent decision involving her own body, including the right to choose life. Personal freedom.

M

At 9:10 a.m. on Monday, August 8, 2022, I received an urgent text from the house manager of the residence at Mar-a-Lago.

"The FBI is outside the house," she wrote. "They are saying we need to leave. The Secret Service is checking the situation. I don't understand what is happening."

At the time, I was in New York City, at a doctor's appointment, and unable to respond immediately. My mind began to race. The FBI? Was there a threat? Fortunately, Donald and Barron were also in New York, so I knew they were safe. Still, I couldn't help worrying about other possibilities—perhaps an issue involving the staff or even a threat to the property itself.

Upon returning home, I contacted Donald and gained insight into the situation. By that point, news of the FBI raid on Mar-a-Lago had gone viral, dominating television and social media. Rather than protecting us, the FBI's actions represented a politically motivated intrusion linked to my husband's personal presidential documents. Watching the helicopter footage of agents surrounding our home from New York, I felt a profound sense of personal violation.

Throughout the day, I remained in communication with Donald, who was in touch with his legal team. Neither of us could believe what was unfolding. A raid on a former president's house, on our home? The reality of a raid on a former president's residence was astonishing and felt more aligned with authoritarian regimes than with the democratic principles of the United States.

I was fully aware of the lengths to which my husband's political adversaries might go, but this development was an unprecedented low.

We could do nothing but wait as agents conducted their search and turned our home upside down. Access to the premises was restricted. In fact, no one was permitted entry, including our lawyers, so we wouldn't know the extent of the search or the potential impact on our home until the operation concluded.

The agents did not leave until 6:30 p.m., having spent nearly ten hours examining every aspect of our home. Upon speaking with my house manager the next day, I learned they had accessed my bedroom, closets, and office, rummaging through my personal items. They even searched Barron's room, apparently looking for Donald's documents.

This invasive process was unwarranted, especially given my thorough efforts to ensure all my official materials were properly transferred to the National Archives and Records Administration (NARA) upon leaving the White House. I had no confidential documents in my possession, no involvement with the West Wing, no knowledge of any classified documents, their locations, or their contents. I planned to return in two weeks to personally see what they had done, so I instructed my house manager to leave everything as she found it.

I maintain my home with meticulous organization, so what greeted me when I walked in was both shocking and deeply upsetting. My belongings—clothes, documents, personal files, and medical records—had been rummaged through, leaving me with a profound sense of violation. The anger I felt was compounded by the realization that strangers had invaded my personal space and sifted through my possessions. I could not be certain whether they had taken any of my belongings. The atmosphere in the house was thick with negative energy, tainted by the intrusion. This act, though carried out by a federal agency supposedly dedicated to our protection, felt like a breach of trust and security.

This invasion of privacy I experienced raised significant concerns: Were my phones hacked? Were my emails and text messages being monitored? What had happened to my rights and freedoms? What else was the government capable of?

As First Lady, I recognized and embraced the responsibilities that came with a public life. I knew that many aspects of my life were beyond my control—my schedule, my safety, my work, all were subject to public scrutiny and belonged to the United States government.

However, returning to civilian life, I had anticipated a degree of privacy and the assurance of due process. Following the raid, I became increasingly concerned about the overall security and safety of our environment.

After years of investigations, attacks, and impeachments, I was accustomed to the relentless opposition against Donald. Yet, I never anticipated an event of this magnitude would unfold in America. This felt personal; it was a profound violation of our family's privacy—impacting not just my husband, but also our son and me.

Growing up under a communist regime, the pervasive surveillance of the state shaped my childhood experience. As a child, I was somewhat shielded from the darker aspects of the system, but its presence loomed in the back of our minds. Conversations with my parents later revealed just how oppressive and invasive the state could be.

My father's fleet of nice cars, a symbol of his success, attracted unwarranted scrutiny. In 1978, someone—a neighbor, perhaps, or a colleague or even a supposed friend—reported to the local police that there was something suspicious about my father's lifestyle. The police escalated the matter to the higher authorities, who opened a file on him and even sent agents to the house to go through his documents, searching for any evidence of criminal activity.

My father was not at home during their visit, so my mother showed them around. In the end, they discovered nothing of interest and departed, appearing quite embarrassed and apologetic.

The investigation amounted to nothing because my father conducted his work with complete integrity and adherence to Slovenia's communist law. However, the case paperwork included a provision stating that if the authorities had found anything criminal, it would have resulted in an automatic one-year prison sentence.

Years later, in a bid to tarnish my father's and my family's reputation, certain "journalists" in Slovenia attempted to exploit this narrative. They unearthed these files and falsely reported that my father had actually been imprisoned, which was entirely false. My father was never found guilty of a crime and was never imprisoned.

Similarly, it has been inaccurately reported that my father was actively involved in the Communist Party. In reality, his membership was a consequence of his high-ranking position and salary at Slovenija Avto. His Communist Party affiliation was a mandatory induction, as the party had implemented an automatic monthly disbursement of a portion of his salary. This arrangement was not reflective of his political beliefs.

The surveillance state in Communist Slovenia serves as a stark reminder of the potential for government overreach. It extended beyond my father, of course; the state monitored almost everyone, spying and gathering information in any way possible. It was a system designed to stifle freedom, instill fear, and keep people powerless. I never imagined such an invasion of privacy and violation of rights could occur in my adoptive country. It was with a tremendous sense of sadness that I realized such unlawful acts were now possible here. Americans need to understand the dangers posed by a federal government that feels entitled to invade our homes and our lives. The possibility of similar abuses occurring domestically demands our attention and action, as we must safeguard our liberties before they are lost forever.

Chapter 18

"Good Luck and Be Safe"

It had been a relatively quiet Saturday in Bedminster. Barron played sports outside. I was working on finishing my project. Around 6 p.m., I turned on the TV to watch Donald's speech but paused it after five minutes. I needed a brief moment of uninterrupted focus to complete my tasks before resuming the rally.

"Are you watching the rally?" My chief of staff said when I picked up, her voice shaky. "Yes, I have it on," I said, "but I paused it. What's going on?"

"I just want to let you know he's okay. He . . . is . . . okay," she said slowly. "But there was a shooting."

I rushed to the TV and pressed play. I couldn't believe what I was seeing. Standing transfixed in front of the television, I watched the chaos unfold: the gunfire, Donald instinctively reaching up to his head, and the immediate response of Secret Service agents shielding him. Though my chief of staff insisted Donald was unharmed, the footage suggested otherwise.

"He's on the ground," I called out. "Are you sure he's okay?"

"I was told he is," she reassured me. "He's on the way to the hospital, but he's fine."

My mind racing, I hung up and immediately dialed Donald. When he didn't answer, I contacted his Secret Service detail. Thankfully, they told me they were already at the hospital and, after what felt like an eternity, put Donald on the line. "I'm okay," he assured me. It was only when I heard his voice that I could finally believe that he really was fine.

Now, Barron rushed in, his faced filled with worry.

"What happened? Is Dad okay?" he asked, breathlessly.

The Secret Service had told him there had been an incident at the rally and that he should go inside.

"He is okay," I told him.

Barron wanted to see what was happening, so we replayed the footage and watched it together. We were both in shock. As we tuned into the news coverage, I felt a deep sense of distress. Can I explain how traumatic it is for a child to witness the attempted murder of his father? The relentless replay of the rally footage on the news only intensified our anxiety. Each time we saw Donald's bloodied face, I had to remind myself that I had actually just spoken to him, heard his voice, and knew that he was safe.

Before Donald announced his first candidacy in 2016, we had talked about the implications of his decision on his and our personal safety. We recognized the inherent risks associated with such a high-profile position, including the potential risk to him, to me, and, hardest to contemplate, even to Barron. We have come to terms with these realities, but the worry never goes away.

As a wife and mother, the safety of my family is a constant concern. Before Donald's arrival in Pennsylvania for the rally, I reminded him, as I always do before his public appearances, "Good luck and be safe. I'll be watching."

Donald was discharged from the hospital after an observation period and returned home to Bedminster at 2 o'clock in the morning. Barron and I felt relieved at seeing him and hugged him.

The next morning, we discussed the Republican National Convention in Milwaukee and the concerns about safety. Donald was adamant in his decision to attend, determined to confront any potential threats. Donald possesses an innate ability to see the positive side of situations. He always stays focused on the fight ahead. The violence he had just experienced actually reinforced his dedication to lead the country toward stability and progress. Within just a few hours, he was on his way to Milwaukee.

In the days that followed that harrowing and surreal event, I found myself reflecting on the sequence of moments that led to my husband's near-tragic brush with fate. Donald's survival that day was nothing short of a miracle. Without a rapid shift to his right in his movement, the shooter's aim would have led to a horrible and tragic outcome.

Reflecting on the multitude of possible scenarios made me consider the fragility of life, and I am grateful that he returned safely to his family that night.

Life is precious and can be lost in an instant. At the rally, attended by thousands, that attempted assassination of my husband claimed the life of a brave firefighter named Corey Comperatore, who shielded his wife and two daughters from the bullets with his body. Two other men sustained serious injuries.

Our nation stands at a pivotal moment. We have a choice: to be torn apart by violence, hatred, and division, or to unite in a spirit of love, kindness, and shared humanity. It is critical that we choose the latter before it is too late.

On the morning of July 14, 2024, I drafted a letter to the American people, the kind of letter I had hoped would never be necessary.

I am thinking of you now, my fellow Americans.

We have always been a unique union. America, the fabric of our gentle nation is tattered, but our courage and common sense must ascend and bring us back together as one. When I watched that violent bullet strike my husband, Donald, I realized my life, and Barron's life, were on the brink of devastating change. I am grateful to the brave Secret Service agents and law enforcement officials who risked their own lives to protect my husband. To the families of the innocent victims who are now suffering from this heinous act, I humbly offer my sincerest sympathy. Your need to summon your inner strength for such a terrible reason saddens me.

A monster who recognized my husband as an inhuman political machine attempted to wring out Donald's passion—his laughter, ingenuity, love of music, and inspiration. The core facets of my husband's life—his human side—were buried below the political machine. Donald, the generous and caring man who I have been with through the best of times and the worst of times.

Let us not forget that differing opinions, policy, and political games are inferior to love. Our personal, structural, and life commitment—until death—is at serious risk. Political concepts are simple when compared to us, human beings.

We are all humans, and fundamentally, instinctively, we want to help one another. American politics are only one vehicle that can uplift our communities. Love, compassion, kindness and empathy are necessities.

And let us remember that when the time comes to look beyond the left and the right, beyond the red and the blue, we all come from families with the passion to fight for a better life together, while we are here, in this earthly realm.

Dawn is here again. Let us reunite. Now.

This morning, ascend above the hate, the vitriol, and the simple-minded ideas that ignite violence. We all want a world where respect is paramount, family is first, and love transcends. We can realize this world again. Each of us must demand to get it back. We must insist that respect fills the cornerstone of our relationships again.

I am thinking of you, my fellow Americans.

The winds of change have arrived. For those of you who cry in support, I thank you. I commend those of you who have reached out beyond the political divide—thank you for remembering that every single politician is a man or a woman with a loving family.

Sincerely,

Melania Trump

PHOTO CREDITS